BEGINNER'S GUIDE TO SMALL COMPUTERS

✓

BEGINNER'S GUIDE TO
SMALL COMPUTERS

Marvin Grosswirth

Updated and with additional material
by Richard Amyx

Dolphin Books
DOUBLEDAY & COMPANY, INC., Garden City, New York
1983

Library of Congress Cataloging in Publication Data

Grosswirth, Marvin, 1931–
    Beginner's guide to small computers.

    1. Microcomputers. I. Amyx, Richard. II. Title.
III. Title: Small computers.
QA76.5.G765   1983   001.64
ISBN 0-385-17931-6
Library of Congress Catalog Card Number: 82–45324

ACKNOWLEDGMENTS

Many people helped in the completion of this book, especially:

Philip H. Dorn, President, Dorn Computer Consultants, Inc., who has been friend, guide, and mentor throughout the project; Harold L. Menzel, System Technical Specialist, Systems and Data Processing, J. C. Penney Co., Inc., an avowed microcomputer enthusiast (and worthy poker adversary) who offered a multitude of insights from the standpoint of a home computer owner and then meticulously ironed out technical wrinkles in the manuscript; Marilyn S. Grosswirth, who checked and criticized the manuscript for clarity and accuracy and who developed the flowchart on page 50; Kathryn Marsala (otherwise known as "The Bronze Goddess"), Technical Information Specialist and Manager of the Technical Information Center at Equitable Life, who made available the resources of the Center and her own considerable research expertise; and representatives of IBM, RCA, Solid State, Commodore Business Machines, Inc., Pertec Computer Corp., Simon/Public Relations, Inc., The Radio Shack, and especially Texas Instruments—all of whom responded to my pleas for help with alacrity, good humor, and a wealth of valuable material.

New York
February 1978

M.G.

Only a dedicated expert could have kept pace with the incredibly rapid changes and advances that have occurred in the world of small computers over the past thirty-six months. Only a uniquely talented writer could have skillfully woven those changes into the original fabric of this book. To have found both in the person of Richard Amyx was a stroke of good fortune for the reader as well as for the author.

New York
February 1983

M.G.

CONTENTS

CONTENTS

INTRODUCTION

It may be safely assumed that you have acquired this book because you are considering, either seriously or frivolously, the acquisition of a home computer. To someone who has no knowledge of computers and is perhaps even somewhat intimidated by them, the prospect of sharing the sanctity of one's home with such a device may appear a little frightening. Relax. In all likelihood, all you probably really need to feel comfortable about the idea of living with a computer is this book. And all you really need to be comfortable with this book is a high school education or its equivalent, and average intelligence. If you are an electronics engineer or would like to become one, take this book back to the store and see if you can get your money back: we are starting from scratch, and you have already passed us by.

Similarly, if you have a particular love for numbers in general and mathematics in particular, you are likely to find this book somewhat unsatisfying. On the other hand, if you have a slight aversion to mathematics, then this book may well prove to be both a comfort and a help: discussions about mathematics have been kept to the barest possible minimum.

One of the unfortunate truisms about computers, regardless of their size, location, or use, is that a considerable and formidable jargon, almost constituting a different language, has grown up about them. Indeed, the computer field has been guilty of some of the worst atrocities ever perpetrated on the English language. Such words as "retrofit" and such expressions as "artificial intelligence" were coined by computer people. On the other hand, the computer field has been known to produce some worthwhile additions to the language: surely "interface" is one of the most useful and expressive verbs to be added to English in recent years. There is no escaping the jargon, and much of it, therefore, is included in this book. There is, at the back of the book, a Glossary, which can be resorted to in moments of stress; however, it will probably not be necessary to refer to it during the actual reading of these pages. When a new term appears, it is in *italics* and immediately defined. If there is a considerable lapse between a word's initial appearance and a subsequent use, that word again appears in italics. Everything is explained in the text, and there are no footnotes to distract or bedevil you. (A once-over perusal of the Glossary is recommended as an easy and painless means of becoming acclimated to the language of the computer world.)

Beginner's Guide to Small Computers is exactly that: a guide. Its main purpose is to help you decide whether a home computer is for you. Its second purpose is to demonstrate that you need not become involved in complex electronics and mathematics to own and enjoy a personal computer. On the other hand, if you do want to plunge into the world of miniaturized circuits and sophisticated mathematical exercises, a personal computer offers the best opportunities for you . . . because chances are that they won't let you play around with the machines at the office.

BEGINNER'S GUIDE TO SMALL COMPUTERS

1

WHAT IS A COMPUTER?

A computer, unless it is broken, never makes a mistake. It is simply incapable of doing so. When a clerk at the local power company or at your favorite department store or in your company's payroll department says, "The computer made a mistake," you have reason to assume that either that person is stupid or thinks you are. *The computer made a mistake* really means that a person or persons operating the computer made a mistake, either by giving the machine incorrect information or by failing to provide it with a proper set of instructions.

Similarly, when some seemingly simple and logical action on your part is thwarted by the statement "The computer won't let us do that," do not blame the machine. Blame instead the insensitive and intransigent nincompoops who, once having programmed the computer to perform certain functions, are unable or unwilling to get their machine to do something else.

A computer is a machine. It performs arithmetic functions. Having performed these functions, it makes comparisons. Built into this machine is the capacity to remember what it has done. The machine also performs logic functions, and it can be given a set of instructions that tell it what it must do and how it

must do it. It can then produce the results that are achieved upon the completion of those instructions. It performs all these things at an incredibly high speed.

From a purely functional point of view, it is the high speed that differentiates the computer from the human brain. Setting aside for a moment the humanistic or humanizing aspects of the brain, it can be seen that there is a considerable similarity between the machine and the human. A person is also capable of doing arithmetic, of making comparisons, and of remembering what he or she has done. And a person can be told what has to be done, how it is to be done and, after following the instructions, produce a desired result.

Consider, for example, a fairly commonplace cost-allocation problem, likely to arise in virtually any business situation. Suppose I have 4 people working for 17 hours at a rate of $4.82 per hour. Suppose further that there is a payroll tax of 11.4 percent. Assume further that the total cost is to be equally divided among three separate projects. What is my total cost? What is my cost per project? With several sharp pencils, a large quantity of paper, and more endurance than I have been known to demonstrate, I would perform the following tasks:

15

(1) Multiply $4 \times 17 \times 4.82$.
(2) Multiply that answer by .114 (11.4%).
(3) Add the result of step (1) to the result of step (2).
(4) Divide that answer by 3.

If the telephone does not ring, if I have had a good night's sleep, and if I come up with the right answers the first time through, I would estimate that solving that problem would take me eight to twelve minutes. However, I have a hand-held calculator (which, as we shall see later, is a kind of a computer) that is a fairly simple one: It has the four basic arithmetic functions of addition, subtraction, multiplication, and division. It also has a "percent" key which makes possible the automatic calculation of percentages. All I need to do, therefore, is press the following keys on my calculator:

$$4 \times 17 \times 4.82 + 11.4\% \div 3 =$$

That operation takes about fifteen seconds. (The answer, if you care, is $365.12 for the total cost, $121.71 for each project.) Fifteen seconds versus eight minutes represents a considerable saving in time; yet, when it comes to computers, hand-held calculators are considered agonizingly slow.

Calculating machines that enable people to rapidly perform computations are by no means a new concept. At some unknown point in antiquity, one or several of our sophisticated ancestors realized that by using some object to represent digits it might be possible to perform computations beyond the limited scope of one's own ten fingers and ten toes. Shells, chicken bones, peach pits, or any number of objects could have been used, but the fact that the word "calculate" is derived from *calculus,* the Latin word for small stone, suggests that pebbles were in great demand. Ultimately, such pebbles or beads were arranged to form the familiar abacus, the first man-made computing device. The abacus was in use for centuries, its decline coinciding more or less with that of the Roman Empire. It was reintroduced in Europe around the year A.D. 1000, but it never regained its earlier popularity. In the Far East, however, its use has continued to this very day.

The abacus is based upon a series of vertical lines on which are strung a number of beads. The first line (counting from the right) represents units. The second line represents tens; the third, hundreds; the fourth, thousands, etc. Running horizontally through the abacus' frame is a bar. The beads above this crossbar represent fives; those below the crossbar represent ones. A Chinese abacus has two beads over the crossbar and five below the crossbar on each line. The *soroban,* the Japanese abacus, is similar in operation but has four beads below the bar and one above. By manipulating the beads, it is possible, with some skill and practice, to make rapid calculations.

In 1642, a French mathematician named Blaise Pascal invented an adding machine based on the principle of the abacus but eliminating the need to move the counters by hand. Pascal's device consisted of several wheels. Each wheel was engraved with the digits 0 through 9 and equipped with a little tab situated near the 9 on the wheel's edge. When the unit's wheel was turned to 0, the little tab engaged the second wheel, turning it to number 1, so that together, the wheels displayed the number 10. When the next—the tens—wheel reached 0, its tab turned the third wheel a notch, displaying 100. And so on. Although Pascal's adding machine was invented over three centuries ago, its principle is still in use in such devices as your car's odometer and the counter on a tape recorder.

Thirty-two years later, a German with the formidable name of Gottfried Wilhelm von Leibnitz made several improvements on Pascal's machine. Thanks to Leibnitz, the device could now multiply and divide as easily as it could add and subtract. In 1850, D. D. Parmalee, an American inventor, devised a system by which properly marked keys turned the wheels, eliminating the need to do so by hand. The addition, years later, of an electric motor to Parmalee's improvement is the grandfather of the familiar adding machine.

In the meantime, there were men of vision looking far beyond the mere functions of addition, subtraction, multiplication, and division. One such forward thinker was the nineteenth-century English mathematician Charles Babbage. In the late-eighteenth century, Joseph Marie Jacquard, a Frenchman, invented the mechanical loom. Jacquard's loom wove fabrics in a variety of patterns based upon "instructions" entered on a series of punched cards. In 1833, Babbage applied the punched-card concept to a machine he called his "analytical engine." Babbage envisioned a machine capable of performing virtually any mathematical operation. It would have a "memory" that could store numbers. It could make comparisons between the results of the various operations. In short, what Babbage had envisioned was the modern computer. He spent nearly four decades developing his ideas, and ultimately failed because it was impossible to produce the parts required for his machine precisely enough. Although the analytical engine was never built, it incorporated many of the elements of modern computers. What Babbage lacked was electronics.

In 1890, Herman Hollerith, working for the U.S. Census Bureau, devised a series of holes punched into cards representing the digits 0 through 9 and the letters of the alphabet. The principle of the punched card is a simple one. When the card is passed over a series of electrical contacts, the hole permits the completion of an electrical circuit. The arrangement of those electrical circuits that have been com-

pleted represents a set of instructions. The code developed by Hollerith (called, not surprisingly, the Hollerith code) is still being used.

With the Hollerith method, computerization was well on the way. In 1890, the Census Bureau used punched cards to classify the American population, cutting by two thirds the time it had taken to do the same thing ten years earlier. The success of the Census Bureau inspired other government uses for the punched-card method; and in 1911, International Business Machines (IBM) was born out of the union between a company that manufactured Hollerith's equipment and a competitive firm.

As the use of electricity became more sophisticated and technology improved, calculating machines also improved. The Burroughs adding machine made its first appearance in 1885, and in 1917, just in time for the American entry into World War I, a calculator that could add, subtract, multiply, and divide came on the scene. In 1925, Vannevar Bush, an American electrical engineer, together with his colleagues, built a machine that could solve differential equations. In 1937, Howard Aiken, of Harvard University, using Babbage's principles, envisioned a completely automatic electromechanical computer.

Through the combined efforts of the Harvard geniuses and IBM, the Automatic Sequence Controlled Calculator was brought to life in 1944. Christened the MARK I, it could perform addition, multiplication, subtraction, and division in any specified sequence. The MARK I could store and regurgitate tables of results it had previously computed. Information was fed into the MARK I by punched cards and by the proper setting of certain switches; MARK I typed its answers out on a typewriter or punched them onto cards. It took the system about three seconds to creak out a typical multiplication. The machine weighed about five tons; its memory contained

BEGINNER'S GUIDE TO SMALL COMPUTERS

over three thousand electromechanical relays. MARK I survived for fifteen years and was finally retired from service in 1959. Portions of its innards may be viewed at the Smithsonian Institution, in Washington.

Roughly coinciding with Professor Aiken's development of the MARK I, John P. Eckert and John W. Mauchly, at the University of Pennsylvania, struck upon the concept of using electronics as a means of obtaining the high speeds necessary to process the enormous quantities of data on ballistics and meteorological studies that were their responsibility. They designed the Electronic Numerical Integrator and Computer, which was promptly labeled by its initials, ENIAC. Their machine contained some eighteen thousand vacuum tubes, of which one was expected to fail approximately every seven-and-a-half minutes. Before very long, however, specially designed vacuum tubes enabled ENIAC to run for several days in succession without having to have one or more of its tubes replaced. ENIAC was fast: it could multiply in 2.8 milliseconds and add in 0.2 millisecond. (A millisecond is a thousandth of a second.) For all its speed, however, it was monstrous by today's standards. In *Asimov's Guide to Science,* author Isaac Asimov writes: "Whereas ENIAC weighed thirty tons and took up 1,500 square feet of floor space, the equivalent computer today—using switching units far smaller, faster, and more reliable than the old vacuum tubes—could be built into an object the size of a refrigerator." But that was written in 1972. A mere five years later, it was possible and practical to manufacture a computer with ENIAC's capability contained in a unit that fits comfortably on a tabletop.

ENIAC was the progenitor of the modern computer. The history of development from ENIAC to computers for home use is essentially a chronology of electronic innovation, refinement, and improved production methods, as we shall see in Chapter 4.

With dismaying frequency, computers are compared to the human brain. The comparison is justified only to an extent. At this very moment, you are receiving information by reading this book. That information enters your brain and may proceed along any one of several paths. It may be placed in your memory for early retrieval. For example, if you are planning to buy a computer tomorrow, then you will want to recall what you have learned today about home computers. If, however, you do not plan to purchase a computer for some time, then the information you are now receiving may be placed in another "compartment" of your memory, which, for want of a better word, we can call "storage." At some later date, you may want to retrieve that information from storage. At the same time, your brain contains other data relevant to your purchase of a computer. You know whether you have the financial resources to buy one. You know whether you have the space to accommodate one. You know (or will know by the time you finish this book) how much technical dexterity will be required to operate one and how much you are capable of delivering. When you have all the information necessary for making a decision, you will compare pieces of data and arrive at an intelligent conclusion. For example, you will compare the size of a computer with the space you have available for it and, on the basis of that comparison, determine whether you have room for the machine. You will compare the cost of the machine with the amount of money you have available and determine whether you can afford to buy it. You will have performed, in other words, what in the computer world is referred to as *data processing*. Data processing means taking a quantity of information—*data* —and performing a systematic and sequential series of operations, either mathematically or logically or both. In other words, processing the data.

A computer also processes data. It can take

information and, by performing mathematical and/or logical operations, arrive at a conclusion and make a decision. For example, if you feed into the computer the price of the device you are interested in buying and your total financial resources, and then feed in your total expenses, the computer will be able to add all of your expenses, deduct that total from your available financial resources, compare the remainder with the price of the computer you want to buy, and then make a decision. If there is enough left over, the computer will tell you to go out and buy. If there is not enough left over, the computer will tell you not to buy. So far, so good: as we discussed earlier, the computer can do what the human brain can do, except much faster.

Thus the computer may be said to be equivalent to a human brain. However, the computer has no mind. More than one commentator has described a computer as an idiot. It can do only what it is told to do and only how it is told to do it. If you are trying to decide, for example, between the purchase of an encyclopedia and a home computer, no calculating machine, however sophisticated, can tell you which is better for furthering the education of your children or honing their intellects.

One of the sadder absurdities that has evolved with the evolution of computer technology is computer crime. It has often been stated that the computer is the perfect partner in crime because it has no morals, it can keep a secret, it does exactly what it is told, and it has no loyalty. In every instance in which crime by computer has been brought to light, the exposure was the result of human rather than machine failure.

Despite science fiction to the contrary, the likelihood of computers taking over the world is slim at best. The computer is a tool of humankind. It is an efficient tool and one that has certainly changed everyone's life.

As the cliché so aptly puts it, the computer's usefulness for good or evil depends not on the machine, but on who is manipulating it.

2

HOW COMPUTERS WORK

● **The Basic Elements**

Let's carry our analogy between computer and human affairs just a bit farther. The complex machine we call a computer can be pictured as consisting of only four basic units: (1) the central processing unit, (2) memory, (3) storage, and (4) input and output (I/O) devices.

The *central processing unit,* or, as it is more familiarly known, the *CPU,* is the computer's "brain." Its name is actually quite descriptive of its function. It is inside the CPU that instructions are decoded and the arithmetic is done. The CPU also controls the functioning of the other parts of the computer.

The computer's *memory* can be likened to the human brain: just as the human brain contains a collection of information that a person can immediately draw upon for use, so the computer's memory holds a certain amount of information that the CPU can directly inspect, modify if required, and store again for later use; and just as the human brain can learn by taking in new information, so can the computer's memory tuck away new information coming in from an input device or resulting from the internal manipulation of data.

Information in *storage* is not directly accessible in memory (a human's or a computer's), but is situated in some known place. In the case of a human, the known place may be the living-room bookshelf, the public library, or another human's brain. In the case of a computer, the known place will usually be on a magnetic tape, disk, or diskette, or perhaps on something like punched cards.

Input and *output* are, in effect, the eyes, ears, and mouth of the computers. An *input device* is one that enables you to put instructions and information—or data—into the computer. Typically, an input device consists of a typewriter-like keyboard, a keypad similar to that of a hand-held calculator or a push-button telephone, a tape reader, or any of various other kinds of devices.

An *output device* is one the computer uses to relay its findings: a video screen, a typewriter, a printer, or some other device. Obviously, some of these objects can be used for both input and output. Frequently, therefore, input and output devices are categorized together and indicated by the symbol *I/O*. One of the more offensive linguistic abominations perpetrated by the computer industry is the use of "input" and "output" as verbs. Thus, one inputs data to the computer, which then outputs the result. (I/O devices, also known as *peripherals,* are discussed at greater length in the next chapter.)

• The Binary System

If the CPU is the brain of the computer, then electricity is its blood. Electricity always travels in a complete circuit. It emanates from a source, travels through some "resistance," and returns to the source. "Resistance" can be visualized as an impediment in the circuit that draws off some of the electricity for the performance of some function. For example, if you are reading this book by artificial light, the lamp is a resistance through which the electricity must flow. When you turn off the lamp by flipping a switch, you break the circuit. A computer contains thousands of tiny circuits, each of which is used to perform a specific function. Some circuits are used for addition, some for subtraction; others hold instructions or retain numbers. The function and location of each circuit are "known" by the CPU.

The fact that electricity flows in a circuit is basic to the operation of a computer and to the conveyance of information. Let us have another look at your reading lamp. Your lamp is either on or off. If it is on, the bulb is glowing and you can tell that the lamp is on. If it is off, the bulb is dark and you know that the lamp is off. That is, of course, simple almost to the point of idiocy. But as you will soon see, that actually provides a considerable amount of data. If the bulb were not in the lamp, you could still tell whether it was on or off by the position of the switch. If the switch were inaccessible, and there were no bulb in the lamp, you could *still* determine whether the lamp was on or off by inserting your finger in the socket (although whether the informa-

tion is worth the price is something else again).

Now, let us assume that you have not one, but four reading lamps neatly arranged in a straight line. In your imagination, label the lamp at the extreme right with the number 1. Label the next lamp number 2, the next number 4, and the one at the extreme left number 8. Turn off all the lamps. You should now have an arrangement approximately resembling this sketch:

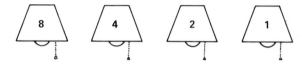

Now you can represent any of the four digits shown merely by turning on the appropriate lamp. You can also represent several other values by turning on combinations of lamps. For example, you could represent the value of 3 by turning on lamps 1 and 2, the value of 10 by turning on lamps 8 and 2, the value of 12 by turning on lamps 8 and 4, the value of 15 by turning on all the lamps, etc. What we have here, then, are definitions of two essential aspects to the function of a computer. First, we have a working definition of *electronics.* This often-used and much-abused word simply means the transmittal of information by means of electricity. The on-off states of the lamps also give us the basis for a numbering system known as *binary notation.* Before delving into the binary system, it may be useful to briefly review our more common method of numbering, the decimal system.

The *decimal system* is a base-10 system. That means that it is based on the number 10. Consider, for exanple, the number 4,376. We know, from its place in that series, that the 6 represents units; in other words, it is in the 1's column. Immediately to the left is the 10's column, so the 7 is really 7 times 10, or 70. The 3 is in the 100's column and represents

300, and the 4 is in the 1,000's column and represents 4,000. Should it be necessary to do so, we could, theoretically, continue adding digits to the left of the 4, and each successive place would represent a value ten times greater than the one immediately preceding it. With that in mind, let us return to the binary system.

Binary means base-2; 2 is the only number base that a device which depends on the flow of electricity can use, because electricity is either on or off; therefore, those are the only two states to which values can be assigned. To be specific, if we go back to our lamps, we can say that when a lamp is on, it has a value of 1. When it is off, it has a value of 0. In the decimal system, each place has a value ten times greater than the place immediately preceding it. In the binary system, each place has a value double the one preceding it. Presumably, therefore, we could continue to add to our string of lamps. A lamp to the left of the one numbered 8 would have a value of 16, a lamp to the left of that would have a value of 32, the next one would have a value of 64, and so on.

Now let's transfer this concept to the innards of a computer. Obviously, a computer packed full of reading lamps is impractical. There is instead an arrangement of electrical impulses that are turned on or off depending upon the number to be represented. If "off" means 0 and "on" means 1, then a number can be represented by arranging ones and zeros accordingly. For example, the binary character 0110 represents the value of 6. The 0 on the extreme right, being "off," has no value. The 1 in the place second from the right has a value of 2. The 1 to the left of that has a value of 4, and the 0 at the extreme left has no value. The 4 and the 2 equal 6. That configuration, 0110, always means 6 to the computer. The computer can store it, can use it to perform arithmetic functions, shift it around as necessary, and display it as a 6.

These representations (on = 1, off = 0) are called *bits* (contraction for *bi*nary dig*it*). The grouping of bits, such as 0110 to represent the number 6, is called a *character*.

The number of bits in a character never changes. In any given computer, all the characters have the same number of bits. Establishing the number of bits in a character produces a *code*—i.e., a set of characters each of which has a fixed number of bits. This code is, in effect, the computer's own language, the medium through which the computer talks to itself. In a sense, the code can be compared to an alphabet. In our alphabet, we use the symbol *b* to represent a certain sound. To effectively communicate in our language, that symbol must always represent that sound. In some other alphabet, this same sound may be represented by a completely different symbol, but it must be consistent in its representation within that alphabet and any language that uses that alphabet. So an alphabet is, after all, just another form of code.

By combining the principle of "on" representing 1 and "off" representing 0 with the binary number system, we see that a four-bit character can represent 0 through 15, or 0000 through 1111. But, in our decimal system, ten single-place digits—0 through 9—are used. To enable a computer to use the binary system to represent the decimal system, a set of characters—a code—was derived from the binary system and used to convey the digital values of the decimal system. It is called, not surprisingly, *Binary Coded Decimal,* or *BCD*. BCD uses four bits representing 1, 2, 4, and 8 (remember the lamps?) and two "zone bits," which allow the coding of addition characters.

But BCD provides only sixty-four characters: the digits 0 through 9, the alphabet, punctuation, and some special-purpose characters. As a code, the BCD is adequate but somewhat limiting.

As a result, a method was found to extend

the codes. One such extended code is the *Extended Binary Coded Decimal Interchange.* (Surely it will not surprise you by now to learn that this is abbreviated as EBCDIC, and pronounced EBB-SEE-DIK.) The EBCDIC code uses two four-bit characters in tandem for each representation. The first four bits constitute a *classification character.* The other four bits are used for the character itself. There are sixteen classifications, each of which contains sixteen characters, for a total of 256 characters. When the computer "reads" the classification character, it can tell what the next four bits will represent. Thus, a four-bit character may represent a digit or a letter or a mathematical function. Its specific application is determined by the classification character that precedes it.

This method of extended coding provides for 52 alphabetical characters (the alphabet in upper and lower case), the digits 0 through 9, punctuation and other signs and symbols, and various controls and directions within the central processing unit. In all, some 150 characters are coded in EBCDIC, leaving the remaining 106 characters available for a wide variety of special functions.

Strictly speaking, the bit patterns in the EBCDIC are not exactly characters, because they each consist of two elements: the classification function and the information function. This type of character is known as a *byte.* (I have no idea why.)

Sometimes, a computer moves around a unit consisting of half a byte, or four bits. In what can only be seen as an excess of cuteness, these half bytes are referred to as *nibbles* (except by those who can never leave bad enough alone and prefer *nybbles*).

The EBCDIC code was developed by IBM for its System/360 computer, a system in extensive use in commerce and industry. It is, therefore, one of the most popular, but by no means the only, code in existence.

Codes are concerned chiefly with the inner workings of the machinery, so the chances of your becoming directly involved with them are somewhat remote. If you become intimate with your computer and want to make some changes or adjustments in the code, the manufacturer of the equipment can undoubtedly supply you with the information you will need.

Number Systems Equivalents

Decimal	Binary	Hexadecimal
0	0000	0
1	0001	1
2	0010	2
3	0011	3
4	0100	4
5	0101	5
6	0110	6
7	0111	7
8	1000	8
9	1001	9
10	1010	A
11	1011	B
12	1100	C
13	1101	D
14	1110	E
15	1111	F

There is one other numbering system you ought to know about, although at first you will probably not be using it. Clearly, the binary numbering system leaves considerable room for error, particularly in long numbers, in which the 1's and 0's can easily become transposed and such transposition is likely to go undetected. To minimize such errors and to increase the speed with which programs can be written, the *hexadecimal* (base-16) numbering system is used. A table summarizing the equivalents in decimal, binary, and hexadecimal number systems is shown above. As you can see, the hexadecimal system employs the letters A through F in addition to digits. In computer notation, hexadecimal numbers are usually represented with an "H" suffix, as

ASCII Code Conversion Chart

SECOND HEXADECIMAL DIGIT

		0	1	2	3	4	5	6	7	8	9	A	B	C	D	E	F
	0	*NUL	SOH	STX	ETX	EOT	ENQ	ACK	BEL	BS	HT	LF	VT	FF	CR	CO	SI*
	1	*DLE	DC1	DC2	DC3	DC4	NAK	SYN	ETB	CAN	EM	SUB	ESC	FS	GS	ES	US*
	2	SP	!	"	#	$	%	&	'	(	)	*	+	,	-	.	/
	3	0	1	2	3	4	5	6	7	8	9	:	;	<	=	>	?
	4	@	A	B	C	D	E	F	G	H	I	J	K	L	M	N	O
	5	P	Q	R	S	T	U	V	W	X	Y	Z	[	\	]		—
	6	\	a	b	c	d	e	f	g	h	i	j	k	l	m	n	o
	7	p	q	r	s	t	u	v	w	x	y	z	‹		›	∿	DEL

FIRST HEXADECIMAL DIGIT

in 87ADH, or in a special format that looks like this: 'x'87AD.

The hexadecimal system is used as a kind of shorthand for writing binary numbers.

Several books prepared for computer hobbyists and enthusiasts discuss the hexadecimal numbering system in some detail. The likelihood of your having to trouble yourself with such mathematical niceties, however, is slim, at least in the early stages of your involvement with your own home computer.

A particularly important code is the *ASCII* (for American Standard Code for Information Interchange). This code is used by computers to permit the interchange between the I/O devices and the central processing unit. ASCII can be written in several ways. The chart above shows the ASCII written in the hexadecimal numbering system, but it can be converted to the binary or the decimal numbering system.

Thus, to translate the letter W into ASCII code, look on the chart for the letter W. You will find that it is in horizontal row 5. Vertically on the chart it is equal to the number 7 under Second Hexadecimal Digit, so that the letter W written in ASCII code is 57. Reversing the process, if we see the ASCII code 3D, by checking the above chart, we find that that represents an equals sign (=).

The full ASCII code comprises 128 units, including alphanumerics, punctuation, and special symbols. *Alphanumerics,* as the construction of the word suggests, is computerese for letters and numbers. In the case of the ASCII code, the alphanumerics are all the letters of the alphabet in both upper and lower case, and the digits 0 through 9.

● **The Central Processing Unit (CPU)**

The central processing unit has two main components. One is the *control unit,* and the other is the *arithmetic/logic unit.*

The *control unit* can reasonably be compared with the human brain. If you strike your thumb with a hammer, a signal is transmitted from the injured area to the brain, and in rapid, split-second succession, you drop the hammer, jerk your thumb away, and emit a sound that could be anything from *Ouch!* to some unprintable expletive. All of that is essentially automatic and requires no effort on your part; the brain is "programmed" to have your body react in such a manner. Now, as you gaze at your throbbing thumb, you decided that the pain and swelling might be eased by cold running water. You go into the kitchen, turn on the tap, and plunge your thumb into the soothing stream. Each one of

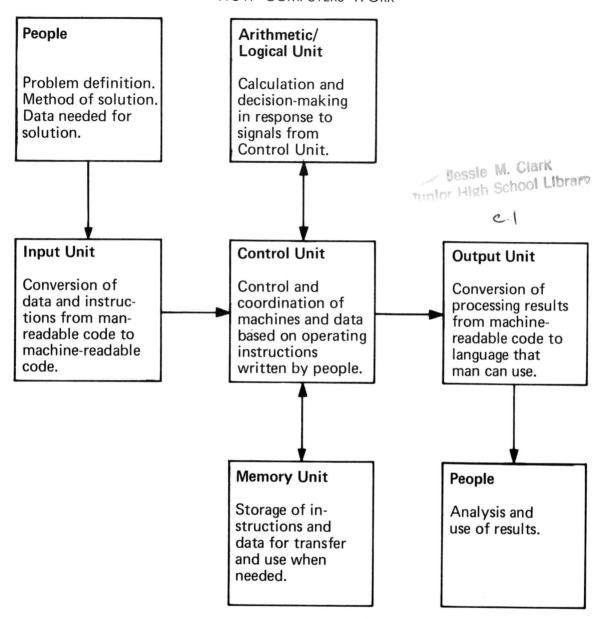

A block diagram of a computer system. The basics
shown here are the same for any system, regardless
of size or capacity. Courtesy IBM.

those steps, from the decision to the final action, is controlled within your brain.

In approximately the same way, the control unit of the CPU controls the actions, both automatic and nonautomatic, of the computer.

The control unit in the computer receives and "understands" the orders and instructions it receives. It then converts those orders and instructions into action, turning various devices on and off, moving information around within the system, and controlling and directing the arithmetic/logic unit.

The *arithmetic/logic* (ALU) unit contains all the circuits of a central processing unit in which, as the name suggests, the mathematical and logical operations are performed. These are known as *logic circuits*. The arithmetic portion of this unit controls addition, subtraction, multiplication, division, square-root calculations, the solving of exponential problems, dealing with trigonometric functions, etc.

The logic unit consists primarily of the *accumulator*. Essentially, the accumulator is a kind of holding area. It is a temporary memory for information coming into the logic unit from the main storage. It also retains answers that are produced by the adders (which we will get to in a moment). Partial answers that must be retained while working out computations are also temporarily stored in the accumulator.

Also situated among the logic circuits are the *adders*. The adder's role is almost explained by its name, but it is not merely an adding machine. Its function is to add the bits coming from the accumulator to those coming from main memory and produce a 1 or a 0, depending upon the identity of the received bit.

Within the control unit and the arithmetic/logic unit there are *registers*, devices used for temporary storage. The bits that have been taken from memory and that will be returned to memory are held in the registers.

● **Memory**

Perhaps the easiest way to understand a computer's memory is to compare it with human memory.

1. There is probably a limit to the number of memory cells in the human brain, but it is generally acknowledged that that limit has never been reached. We know that only a small portion of the brain is actually used, and that with sufficient training or motivation, additional cells can be brought into use. This is demonstrated by the seemingly unlimited capacity to learn. The very fact that you are now reading a book about a subject with which you are probably unfamiliar constitutes your recognition of the existence within your brain of unused memory cells.

A computer's memory, on the other hand, is very limited indeed. Its memory cells are measurable and expressed as quantities of bytes. Thus, using the symbol K to represent one thousand, a home computer is advertised as being equipped with, for example, 4K of memory. That means it has four thousand bytes within its memory system.

2. There seems to be no upper limit to the total amount of data that a human memory can hold. Some people seem to be able to retain more information than others, and there is probably some total capacity beyond which we cannot go, but in general, training and motivation can pack ever more information into most human memories.

In a computer, on the other hand, once the "memory cells"—that is, the bytes—have been loaded with data, not a single shred of additional information can be packed into it. Each bit can hold only one unit of information, and no additional unit of information can be given to it without first removing what is already there. However, in most computer systems it is possible to add memory on to the system by hooking up additional "memory cells."

3. With the exception of the questionable skills of mind readers, there is no way to transmit the information directly from one human memory to another. Data must be removed from memory and translated into some understandable medium, which may consist of words, sounds, pictures, lights, or action.

In theory—and, indeed, sometimes in practice—the fixed memory of one computer can be removed and placed in another, compatible computer. It can also be transmitted from one computer to another over telephone lines.

4. The information stored in a human memory consists of both instructions and data. For example, you know how to tie a shoe, button a coat, balance a checkbook, start a car, etc. Thus, you have a great many sets of instructions in your memory. You also know the name of the President of the United States, the pronunciation of Encyclopaedia Britannica, and your mother's maiden name. Sometimes, what is merely data in one instance can be instructions in another. For example, knowing how to start a car is really only data until and unless you have a car to start.

In a computer, memory also consists of both data and instructions. However, they are not interchangeable, as in the human memory. To a computer, an instruction is an instruction and a piece of information is a piece of information.

There are three types of computer memory; they can be thought of as main memory, long-term memory, and learned memory.

Main memory is the working memory of the computer. Necessary instructions for performing the immediate tasks at hand are taken from storage units and placed in the main memory by the control unit. Information and instructions from the input device are also placed in main memory. When all the data and instructions have been placed in memory, the *accumulator* (the registers that tempo-rarily hold arithmetic and logical results in the ALU) is cleared and the computer goes to work performing its specified task.

Long-term memory is sometimes called *storage*. Its operation is generally slower than main memory and in comparison to the main, or short-term, memory, contains huge quantities of information. That information can be called into use by the control unit of the CPU as it is needed.

Learned memory is essentially a set of carefully detailed instructions that tell the computer exactly what to do. These instructions are called *routines* and are vital to the operation of the computer. If, for example, the computer is instructed to add a column of figures, it must use its learned memory to ascertain the steps required to perform this task. Learned memory is commonly known as *software,* a term that will become increasingly important to the user of a home computer. For example, the chances are excellent that you will be using your computer to work out your personal income tax. There is already available, at least for some computers, a software *program* (a set of instructions) that tells the computer exactly how to complete a Form 1040, as well as some of the more exotic schedules required by the seemingly sadistic denizens of the Internal Revenue Service. Without such software, it would be necessary for you to develop a program showing the machine how to compile the information, perform the calculations, and complete the necessary forms. With the prepackaged software, you need only feed in the specifics of your income for the machine to calculate and tell you just how much trouble you are in with the government. (We shall have more to say about software later.)

There are several types of memory, including *core* (or RAM: random-access memory), *disk,* and *magnetic tape*. For personal computing, however, the two most important types of memory are those on so-called "chips" and tape cassettes. Before discussing these various types, however, it will be helpful to have a somewhat clearer picture of what memory looks like. To do that, let's go through a quick review:

Within the computer, binary digits are represented by "on" and "off"—more correctly, "pulse" and "no-pulse," referring to electrical pulses. The "on," or "pulse," is a 1; the "off," or "no-pulse," is a 0. These binary digits are called *bits*. Eight of these bits are combined to form a *character,* and these characters are called *bytes.* Now, these characters, in turn, must be combined to form a *word.* A word, therefore, consists of a given number of characters or bytes; the specific number varies with the specific computer. Thus, one computer may use a two-byte word, another a four-byte word, etc. The computer treats each word as a single working unit, so when data is transported from one part of the computer to another, it is moved in the form of words.

Now let's return to our discussion of memory. Computer memory can be visualized as an array of tiny compartments. Each compartment carries a pertinent label, known as its *address.* The memory address is very similar to your own home address. Because it is always the same, anyone who *has* to know where to find your house *can* know where to find it. Similarly, because the memory address is always the same, the control unit always knows where to find it and can put into the compartment whatever must go there or take out of it whatever has been stored there.

If you are still visualizing the array of tiny compartments, then you are probably seeing them as a kind of honeycomb hanging somewhere in the air. Let's bring that image down to earth by defining a few basic terms.

Random-Access Memory (RAM). RAM, which is the equivalent of core memory in large computers, makes up the main memory and learned memory mentioned earlier. While it is called "random access" to distinguish it from a sequentially accessed type of memory, that distinction is of no importance to us here. The import of RAM for us is that it stores binary information in a way that is directly understandable by the CPU. When the CPU is given an address in RAM, it can instantly pluck the information from RAM and put it into use. RAM is discussed in a little more detail below, in the section on "chips."

Disks. Disks, as their name implies, are flat, circular pieces of aluminum, ten to twelve inches in diameter, coated with an iron-oxide magnetic recording material similar to that used on any magnetic tape. Information is written on them and read from them by means of a movable head that works just like the RECORD and PLAY BACK heads on a tape recorder. The disk and its head function something like a phonograph record and its tone arm, the main difference being that the disk head, rather than having to follow a groove from beginning to end, can be directed to specific locations on the disk. Very large amounts of information—on the order of tens of millions of bytes—can be stored on disks and rapidly retrieved.

A variation of the disk is the "floppy" disk (so called because it is flexible), or diskette. Simpler technology makes the floppy disk cheaper than the metal disk used by the large computers, but it is also slower. If a home computer uses disk memory, it will almost certainly be the floppy-disk type.

Chips. In home computers, the most commonly used type of memory is the semiconductor chip. These are small, relatively inexpensive, and capable of packing monumental quantities of information into an astonishingly small space. One tenth of a square inch can often contain over four thousand bits.

We will have more to say about semiconductors and chips in Chapter 4. For this discussion, however, it is important to remember that the chief advantage of a chip is its capability of providing *random-access memory* (*RAM*). To reach the little compartments—the *addresses*—in memory, it could be necessary to go through each little compartment as it occurs in sequence, extracting information whenever the wanted compartment is reached. As far as computers are concerned, such a process can be extremely slow. The random-access memory chip, however, makes random access possible at relatively low cost and greatly increases the speed with which the equipment operates.

Read-Only Memory (*ROM*). As explained earlier, a computer must have a set of instructions to perform its functions. These sets of instructions are called *software*. By employing certain recently developed manufacturing techniques, manufacturers can permanently "engrave" these instructions onto a semiconductor chip. Inasmuch as the memory cannot be erased so that additional information or other information can then be put into it, this is known as a *read-only memory* (*ROM*). ROM is not exactly *hardware,* the computer industry's term for the machine itself and all its physical components: metal, plastic, glass, etc. Nor is it *software,* because, strictly speaking, software can be changed. Someone, therefore, devised the rather clever and appropriate designation of *firmware.* (These analogies, however, can sometimes be carried too far: at least one writer has actually referred to the human brain as "wetware.") The book you are now reading is, in a sense, firmware: it can be removed from being accessed by the "computer" in your head and instantly become irrelevant, but the book itself cannot be changed without destroying it.

One of the chief differences between ROM and RAM is that ROM retains its input indefinitely, whereas RAM, in a home computer, will "forget" the data that has been put into it as soon as the power is turned off.

Cassettes. For personal computing, the tape cassette—the kind used in tape recorders—is one of the best types of memory available. It is inexpensive, and an ordinary tape recorder can be hooked up to the computer for input. The data to be stored is converted into audio tones, which are then recorded on the tape. When the information is required, it is "played back" and reconverted to electrical impulses. The chief disadvantage of tape cassettes is that they cannot be randomly accessed. This means that data must be read in sequence, and sometimes a great deal of data may have to be gone through to arrive at the particular piece of information that is wanted. Retrieval, therefore, takes much longer than it would with diskettes. Thus, tape cassettes are most useful when large quantities of data are to be read and processed as part of a continuing program, or when such programs need to be stored so that they can later be read into memory. When purchasing your personal computing equipment, care should be taken to see that systems using tape cassettes are supported by reasonable amounts of available software.

There is another advantage to tape cassettes, one that is shared by floppy disks and some other types of memory: it is memory that is transferable. If I record a message on my tape recorder, remove the cassette, and mail the cassette to you, you can place that cassette in your tape recorder and receive that message—always provided, of course, that we speak the same language. The same holds true for computers. As long as the equipment can accept the memory, and as long as the computers speak the same language, then, in effect, computers can "talk" to each other.

While that is an important and interesting concept, it is more important that computers communicate with the people using them. All of that arithmetic, logic, calculating, comparing—in short, *data processing*—going on inside the central processing unit is of little value until and unless the computer can tell us what is going on and what it knows.

3

THE COMPUTER SPEAKS

We have been talking at some length about giving instructions and information to a computer. We have also discussed what the computer can tell us. But how is this information conveyed to and from that electronic wonder? As already mentioned, this communication with the computer is done through input/output (I/O) devices.

Sophisticated computer systems often use some rather exotic input devices, sometimes consisting of a complexity of electronic circuitry that can perform such minor miracles as transforming the configurations of the human body into bits and bytes.

• I/O Ports

A port is a kind of staging area. Data from an input device passes through the port and is processed for use by the computer. Similarly, the computer's output first passes through the port, where it is prepared for the output device. In home computers, most ports are used for both input and output and are, therefore, called I/O ports.

There are two kinds of I/O port. The *serial* port receives data serially—that is, one bit at a time—and feeds it into the computer that

way. Processed data is returned to the output device in the same way: one bit at a time. Continuing efforts to reduce the processing time have led to the development of the *parallel* port, which handles data a byte at a time—that is, eight bits in a simultaneous (parallel) way.

This parallel input and output of data is performed by a group of electrical conductors capable of carrying several electronic impulses simultaneously, usually to various parts of the computer. This arrangement is called a *bus*. The electrical conductors can be wires or copper traces, but in home computers, they are likely to consist of a printed circuit board. Buses are used for a number of functions within the computer. Where several buses are used together, it is called a *bus system*. The parallel I/O port consists of a data bus plus the so-called *handshake* signal, which establishes synchronization between the I/O device and the central processing unit.

At this point, it is probably useful to introduce the word *peripheral*. The word is used as both a noun and an adjective. For example, the tape recorder that is used to transfer data from the cassette to the computer is outside of —that is, peripheral to—the computer. It is, therefore, correctly called a peripheral.

*Radio Shack's TRS-80 Model III, a complete,
self-contained, ready-to-plug-in system. Courtesy
Radio Shack, a Division of Tandy Corp.*

• Input

The input device most commonly used with a personal computer is a keyboard. If you have a push-button telephone, then you are already acquainted with one type of keyboard that is often used. Such keyboards permit the entry not only of data but of programs. But as is immediately obvious, it is limited only to entries made by digits and a few symbols. (A hand-held calculator has a similar keyboard.) Such keyboards are always used together with a display, so that the operator can check on the entries as they are being made. Frequently, this type of keyboard is called a *keypad,* to distinguish it from typewriter-like keyboards.

By far the most common type of keyboard is one that resembles a typewriter. This permits the entry of data and instructions through the use of words and letters. This keyboard is also usually hooked up to some sort of display, so that the data can be viewed as it is being entered. That display will also be used for the output, which is why input/output devices are generally discussed as units.

If you have looked at some personal computers, particularly one that has been put together by a hobbyist, you may have noticed that on the computer's front panel there are a number of switches. These switches provide for the entry of data, literally on a bit-by-bit basis, by turning a series of those switches on or off. This is known as *binary key input*. It usually comes as part of a kit, along with instructions for its construction and use. Its chief advantage is its low cost: it is probably cheaper than just about any other input method. Whether the saving is worth the trouble can be determined only by the user's interest in electronics, desire for and affinity toward putting things together, and willingness to spend a lot of time with a hot soldering iron.

• Output

There are several types of output devices. Most people have some familiarity with all of them: video displays, printers, and audio devices.

Video displays. Perhaps the most popular device for home computers—particularly those that are self-contained, ready-to-use systems that need only be purchased, taken home, and plugged in—are the display terminals that look like television screens. A TV screen is actually the visible surface of a large and complicated piece of electronic apparatus known as a *cathode-ray tube (CRT)*, and it is this same tube that is used for the video displays that are hooked up to computers. They are, therefore, commonly known as CRT terminals or CRT I/O devices—or simply CRTs.

The chief advantage of the video display terminal is its dual function as an I/O device. It not only displays input as it is being put in; it also provides the readout for the computer's output.

If you purchase a home computer system that does not come with a video display terminal, there are several ways of adding one on. The simplest is to purchase a terminal that comes equipped with a keyboard. As the data is keyed on the keyboard, it is displayed on the screen. When the user determines that the information displayed on the screen is correct, the appropriate key is pressed and the computer begins processing the data. Computer hobbyists who enjoy putting things together can, of course, purchase CRT terminals and keyboards separately and perform the necessary electrical hookups so that they function with the computer and each other. Complete terminals are also available in kit form.

Many computers are hooked up to a *video monitor*. If you have ever visited a TV studio, you have probably seen monitors in operation. The monitor is the TV set that shows what is going out "over the air" from the studio; it cannot receive signals from other TV stations. Computer hobby stores usually have a wide variety of video monitors, including second-hand ones, available in a broad range of prices.

Many computer hobby stores and mail-order firms sell an *RF* (for "radio frequency") *converter,* which enables the user to hook up a conventional TV set to the computer. The RF converter works through the TV set's antenna terminals. If you choose to purchase such a device—or a kit for constructing one—make certain that the one you buy has been approved by the Federal Communications Commission. You may have to search far and wide for one that has such approval. Unapproved RF converters often interfere with nearby TV reception, incurring the enmity of one's neighbors.

Also available are color video terminals.

Such terminals can be built by the enthusiast, or, with an FCC-approved RF converter, the home color TV set can be connected to the computer. Several *interfaces* (that is, devices that enable the computer to be hooked up to a color TV) are available. They are expensive and, apart from their game-playing and dubious aesthetic qualities, there seems to be little real need for color TV terminals—except, perhaps, in some highly specialized applications.

Almost every major department store and many toy and game dealers now have electronic games, constructed around miniature computers, that can be easily hooked up to a home television set. The hookup usually requires no more than a screwdriver and the ability to read some simple instructions. In such configurations, the home TV set can be considered a peripheral to the computer locked up inside the game. Some TV manufacturers have now begun marketing new models that contain jacks, or plugs, so that the TV games can simply be plugged in. It is only a matter of time—and very little time, at that—until those jacks and plugs will be able to accommodate an *interface* (the adapter that makes two separate pieces of equipment work together) with which you can literally plug your computer into your TV set.

Perhaps the chief disadvantage of a video display terminal is its inability to render a permanent record of what it displays. In computer parlance, such a permanent record is called *hard copy*. (A *printout* is one form of hard copy.) One of the more ingenious methods for obtaining hard copy from a video display terminal is to attach a Polaroid camera to the terminal by means of a bracket. It will not require much in the way of mechanics to arrange the camera so that it can swing out of the way when not in use, and when needed, can be placed in position so that it is the right distance from the screen to include the entire screen in the picture. The camera can also be set at a permanent-focus position. The computer user can then obtain hard copy by taking a Polaroid picture of the video screen.

There are, however, somewhat more efficient and more legible ways of obtaining hard copy.

● Printers

When home computers first began appearing on the mass market, in 1978, printers were much too expensive for most computer buyers. Current technology has, however, made a whole family of dot-matrix printers readily available. The early printers, and other devices adapted for use as computer printers, required a separate typecast element for each character, much like a typewriter. The dot-matrix printers are so named because individual wires in the print head are triggered to produce a dot pattern that creates the letter shape on paper. In other words, one mechanical device creates all the character shapes needed; simpler mechanics means lower prices.

Respectable utility-type dot-matrix printers can now be purchased starting at less than three hundred dollars; from there, prices go up through a rather broad mid-range to around fifteen hundred dollars. But within this range you can select a printer that has several typefaces and sizes (mine, being made in Japan, includes a complete Katakana syllabary), high-resolution graphics or graphic blocks for printing charts and graphs, and such "pretty print" features as boldface, underscoring, and proportional spacing.

Character printers, sometimes called letter-quality printers, which work much like IBM (type-ball) or Olivetti (daisy-wheel) typewriters, still require typecast elements and so cost more than dot-matrix printers, on account of their more complicated mechanical requirements, but they produce crisp, clean impressions suitable for word processing and often indistinguishable from typeset copy. Prices for character printers now start at about sixteen hundred dollars, go through a middle range to around forty-five hundred dollars, then skyrocket to a maximum of ten thousand to eleven thousand dollars for heavy-duty, professional models.

Both dot-matrix and character printers are relatively slow devices in a computer world where time is measured in nanoseconds (a nanosecond is a thousandth of a millionth of a second), clunking along at the rate of 25–80 characters per second. (No matter if that's 300–960 words per minute to a human typist. It's slow.) Line printers, so called because they appear to print a line of type at a time, range in speed from one line per second to several thousand lines per minute, and are most appropriate for massive data processing and reporting. The cheapest, and slowest, line printer goes for about two thousand dollars; prices then ramble on upward to around one hundred thousand dollars.

• Audio Peripherals

When you dial a telephone to get the correct time or when a voice comes on to inform you that you have reached a wrong number, what you are hearing is a computerized voice simulator. Extensive research is now going on to develop computer systems that can "hear" the human voice and receive input that way, but voice-simulated output is already well developed. There are at least two voice simulators on the market designed for use with home computers. They are expensive—in the four hundred dollar range—but prices will probably come down eventually.

Music, on the other hand, is quite another story. There are currently available various peripherals that emit musical tones, and these are relatively low-priced. By programming the computer properly, music—or at least what

purports to be music—can be performed by the computer.

In a certain sense, a home computer can be compared with a camera. The technically skilled amateur photographer can begin with a basic camera body, around which he can construct a system of photography with almost unlimited capabilities. He can buy telephoto lenses, wide-angle lenses, microscope attachments, lighting equipment of varying types, special viewfinders, dozens of filters, testing and checking equipment, motor drives, cable releases, and all kinds of other equipment, attachments, and accessories. The less-skilled photographer may prefer a camera for which equipment, attachments, and accessories are fewer in number but are essentially easier to operate. He may prefer buying self-contained units—such as an electronic flash gun—which can be quickly and easily hooked up to the camera. And finally, there are perhaps millions of photographers content with an Instamatic, a cartridge of film, and a pocketful of flashcubes.

Because of the relative newness of the field, in terms of quantity and sophistication, home computers perhaps offer somewhat less for hobbyists than does the photographic industry. Nevertheless, a wide variety of peripherals and other additions and accessories are available to the computer hobbyist. For example, it is not difficult for a computer hobbyist to begin with a basic 4K-memory computer and gradually build that up to a system with 8K, 12K, 16K, or even more memory.

Similarly, there are people who are not interested in the intricacies of electronics and who, at best, might be prepared to assemble a simple kit, but who really would prefer "add-ons" that need only be plugged into their home computers. Again, many such add-ons are either available now or will be in the very near future.

The decision as to which path to take must,

of course, rest with you. There are two things to be careful about:

First, before you buy any peripheral—be it kit, finished product, or a boxful of wires, plugs, and printed circuits—make certain that what you are purchasing is compatible with the computer you have in your home. Not every video display terminal with a keyboard can be used with every computer.

Second, be certain that the peripheral or accessory that you are buying will perform the job that you want it to, in accordance with your needs. It may be moderately amusing, at least at first, to have a printer rasping or thumping away in your living room (the faster dot-matrix printers make a metallic sound uncomfortably like a dentist's drill) at the push of a button, but if you do not need hard copy, and if the racket is keeping the baby awake, then the printer may prove to be an error in judgment.

Remember the injunction of the first sentence of the first chapter of this book: Computers, unless they are broken, never make mistakes. People, however, frequently do.

4

MICROPROCESSORS

In the late 1950s, researchers at Bell Laboratories developed the transistor, which virtually replaced the old-fashioned vacuum tube. Because of its tiny size, the transistor opened doorways in many areas of electronics that led to miniaturization and, eventually, to subminiaturization. With the advent of the transistor, for example, it became possible to manufacture hearing aids that could be placed directly inside the ear and be virtually invisible. Radios of fairly good range and passable tonal quality could be—and are—made small enough to slip into a shirt pocket.

A further development of the transistor is *large-scale integration* (*LSI*), a process that allows for the arrangement of thousands of nearly microscopic transistors, forming an integrated circuit, on a minuscule slice of silicon. Silicon is a nonmetallic element that is found in the earth's crust. Its chief advantages, from an electronics point of view, are its purity and its function as a *semiconductor*.

If you remember your high school science, then you know that certain materials, such as copper, carry, or "conduct," electricity very well, while other materials, such as rubber and wood, do not conduct electricity at all and are therefore used for insulation against electrical flow. As the term implies, a semiconductor lies somewhere in between. It is neither a particularly good nor a particularly bad conductor. But the "neutrality" of a semiconductor can be altered by implanting certain "impurities," such as atoms of phosphorus or arsenic. This makes possible the introduction of positive and negative charges, which in turn makes it possible to implant transistors. (Exactly how this is done is explained in detail in virtually any decent general science text, such as *Asimov's Guide to Science,* published by Basic Books, and the *Penguin Dictionary of Science,* published by Schocken. Incidentally, although silicon is the one most often used in computers, it is not the only semiconductor; germanium is also well known and widely used in other applications.)

In the mid-1960s, computer technologists developed a method for etching circuitry and logic functions onto a small chip of silicon. A master drawing, about five hundred times larger than the actual chip, is photographically reduced to the required size. Then, employing a method very like photoengraving, the minuscule photograph of the drawing is etched onto the chip. As a result of this circuitry-on-a-chip technique, manufacturers were able to considerably reduce both the cost and the size of computers, giving rise to a new

Surrounded by contact lenses to show relative size,
this tiny chip of silicon, approximately one twentieth
of an inch square, contains a central processing
unit (CPU). Courtesy Texas Instruments.

subindustry: minicomputers. Chip technology also made it possible to produce small, personal "computers" with fixed, nonalterable programs. Hand-held calculators and electronic digital watches are examples of these personal computers.

In 1969, M. E. Hoff, Jr., an engineer for Intel Corporation, a manufacturer of logic and circuitry chips, was placed in charge of a project to produce calculator chips for Busicom, a Japanese company manufacturing calculators. While searching for an economical method of meeting the customer's needs, Mr.

Hoff discovered that he could incorporate the entire central processing unit on a single silicon chip. By attaching two additional chips—one for input and output of data and another for inscribing a program—Mr. Hoff had what amounted to a basic computer. By the time Intel's engineering team worked over Mr. Hoff's invention, it contained 2,250 transistors on a chip that was just under a sixth of an inch in length and an eighth of an inch wide. Each of these transistors was approximately equal to one of the vacuum tubes in the pioneering ENIAC computer. Interestingly, this *micro-*

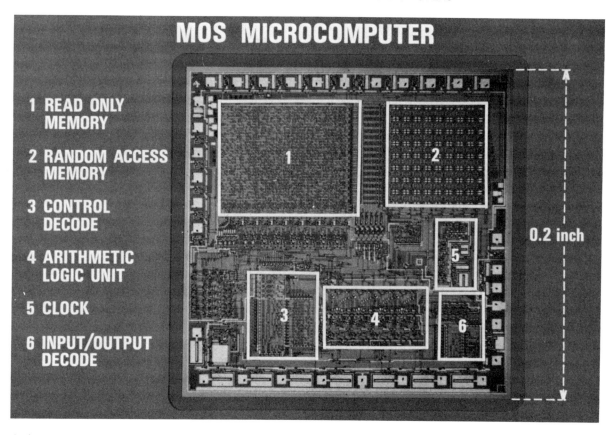

A close-up of a microcomputer on a chip. Courtesy
Texas Instruments.

computer, as it was known, could be mass-produced on the same production lines on which Intel made their memory chips. As a result, the company was now in the business of manufacturing computers.

Micro derives from the Greek word *mikros,* meaning small. (It is often designated by the Greek letter *mu* and written in Greek like this: μ.) The central processing unit (CPU) in a microcomputer is generally referred to as an MPU—a microprocessing unit. Up to now we have been using the terms "home computer" and "personal computer." From now on, we will refer only to microcomputers, because that is what home and personal computers are.

Chips and various other components are mounted on boards made of plastic, known as *printed circuit boards.* The interconnections, consisting of etched foil, or plated conducting pads, are rigid and unalterable. They contain the program and are known as *hard-wired logic.* The typical hand-held calculator (other than the programmable models) is an example of hard-wired logic. The operating program instructions, which consist of the arithmetic functions, are etched permanently in the chips. The application program is, in effect, in the operator's brain. He provides the instructions for performing the specific calculations that achieve the desired results.

Although microprocessors got off to a rather slow start, by the mid-1970s they began to appear everywhere. Among automobile manufacturers, General Motors announced that a microcomputer would be used in its 1977 Oldsmobile Coronado to improve fuel economy by controlling spark-plug firing. Cadillac offers its owners a "trip-master," which computes the driver's estimated arrival time and other useful information. The 1978 Ford Versailles came equipped with microcomputers.

In the meantime, microprocessors are showing up in a wide variety of products. Singer Sewing Machine's Athena 2000 uses an MPU to eliminate some 350 parts that normally go into sewing machines, while at the same time allowing the operator to produce any one of two dozen stitch patterns. Amana, in its Touchmatic Micro Wave Oven, was the first to use a microprocessor in such a device. Other companies quickly followed suit. MPUs are showing up in scanning radio receivers, self-service gas pumps, coin-operated machines that can take your blood pressure, digital clocks and watches, "talking" calculators for the blind, laboratory testing equipment, drink dispensers in bars, refrigerators, clothes washers and dryers, dishwashers, home temperature controls, and dozens of other household products. Those products are cheaper to maintain, because they have fewer moving parts, and they are cheaper to operate, because they make the most efficient use of energy.

In the meantime, many people are having a lot of fun with MPUs. Electronic games that can be easily plugged into home television sets are being sold almost faster than manufacturers can produce them. The MPUs also provide many hours of diversion and amusement for a new species, which, if not native to America, certainly flourishes here: the computer hobbyist. Thanks to the MPU, it is possible to construct a highly sophisticated, reliable, and versatile computer for relatively little money. Perhaps even more interesting, the MPU has made it possible for companies to manufacture and market complete, self-contained, ready-to-plug-in-and-go computers at prices well within the range of the average middle-class American.

The microcomputer *is* the home computer.

5

THE HOME COMPUTER— BASIC COMPONENTS

So far we've been talking, somewhat non-specifically, about various components of computers. We know, for example, that to be regarded as a computer, a system must consist of a central processing unit, memory, and input/output devices. That holds true whether the computer is housed in a collection of formidable-looking steel boxes that occupy half a floor over at corporate headquarters, or whether the computer is situated on a couple of chips of silicon and gives you the time of day or helps you balance your checkbook. Now let's get down to specifics and see what, precisely, ought to be included in your personal computer.

The microprocessor. Contained in one or several integrated circuit chips, it carries the arithmetic/logic unit (ALU), the controls required to operate the computer, and the working registers. (A *register,* you will recall, is a temporary storage location for data.)

Memory. In all likelihood, the printed circuit board (sometimes called *card*) that holds the microprocessing unit (MPU), the version of the home-computer CPU, will also hold some memory. More memory can be added on in almost every case, by means of either additional printed circuit boards or one of several peripheral memory devices.

Data-input device. Almost certainly, this will consist of some sort of keyboard. In a system that the operator has put together from scratch, the keyboard may be a separately purchased mechanism—perhaps from an obsolete terminal—that has been wired into the system. More likely, however, for beginners, the keyboard will be part of a video display terminal or an electric typewriter that has a built-in interface so that it can be hooked up to the computer system. Or it will be one that can be connected to the microcomputer through relatively easy-to-obtain and easy-to-use adapters.

Output device. This is likely to be a video display or some form of printer.

Power supply. Strictly speaking, the power supply is the wall socket into which you plug your computer. However, most home computers operate on direct current (DC), while most household electricity is alternating current (AC). The power supply in a microcomputer system converts the current from AC to DC and maintains a steady, consistent, nonfluctuating flow of electricity. In a microcomputer, the power supply may have to provide varying voltages for differing functions.

If you own a calculator, a transistor radio, or a tape recorder that operates on batteries and have a so-called "AC adapter," then you have some idea of the power supply's function. A typical AC adapter converts 120 volts of alternating current to 6 volts of direct current. The power supply in a microcomputer performs essentially the same function. Most of the time, the power supply is an integral part of the microcomputer's system, but sometimes prices for such computers do not include the cost of the power supply. It is worth making sure that a power supply is either included in the price, or the price for it is given so that you can add it to the total cost.

Software. This consists primarily of the programs used to obtain a particular result through a set of sequential instructions or statements given to the computer. Programs and programming will be discussed at greater length in Chapters 7 and 8.

These are the basic components for every microcomputer system. There are, of course, other devices and facilities that can be added on. Also, almost all the components listed above are in themselves complex arrangements of electronic circuitry. Thus, each part may itself consist of many parts.

You may remember—but let's review it anyway—that within the central processing unit (CPU) is the *control unit*. The control unit receives instructions from the program and, one by one, extracts the appropriate bits from the storage "compartments" in memory. Each instruction is decoded by the control unit or converted from its numeric representation into an appropriate electronic signal.

These signals are then routed to other locations within the microprocessor. The actual work of the microcomputer is performed in other parts of the system, which have received instructions from the control unit as to what data to work on and how and when to do it.

Also situated in the CPU is the *arithmetic/ logic unit* (ALU). Here is where the actual computation—that is, the arithmetic functions —is performed.

The *accumulator* is part of the ALU. It consists of a register in which the arithmetic and logical results are temporarily stored. It is analogous to a chalkboard on which sums and other results are temporarily written down and saved until they are needed, at which time they can be erased.

There are, as you may well imagine, hundreds of other terms applicable to computers that describe devices, electronic circuitry, and functions. Some apply to computers in general, others specifically to microcomputers. Most of the important ones are given in the Glossary, beginning on page 95. How many of these you will be required to know depends entirely on how intimately you plan to become involved with the nuts and bolts of your computing equipment.

But whether you buy a system or build one, whether you are totally ignorant of its inner workings or thoroughly cognizant of every switch and pulse, when you turn your computer on, it will do nothing but hum at you.

It is waiting for you to talk to it.

6

SPEAKING YOUR COMPUTER'S LANGUAGE

All computers, regardless of size, capacity, cost, function, simplicity, complexity, or utility, have one thing in common: way down deep inside the bowels of the machine, where all the work is done, electrical pulses are being turned on or off. A pulse represents binary digit 1; a no-pulse represents binary digit 0. All information that is fed into the computer, whether operating instructions or data, ultimately must be reduced to the pulse/no-pulse "language" of the computer.

At first, the only way computers could be programmed was to write the program using a series of binary numbers. (A *program,* you may recall, is a list of instructions or statements, written in sequence, that will result in the computer's performance of a particular function or task.) Understandably, people who could do such things were regarded with awe and reverence, intermingled with a little suspicion. The opportunity for error was enormous.

Before long, it was realized that if a computer could be programmed to perform certain functions, then one of those functions could be the translation from a less complicated (to humans) language into the binary lingo of the machine. The result of that inspiration was *assembly language* and programs

called *assemblers.* Assembly language consists of *mnemonics,* made up of combinations of letters. Each mnemonic represents a computer instruction. The assembler program translates the assembly language into the binary number system for the computer.

It was only a relatively short step to the development of so-called *high-level languages.* Some of these languages come very close to plain English. Among the more popular are *COBOL* (an acronym for *Co*mmon *B*usiness-*O*riented *L*anguage), a language that requires only a perfunctory familiarity with the internal workings of a computer. If the programmer understands the rules involved in organizing a COBOL program, he can write such a program with little difficulty and, with some adjustments, it will run on any computer equipped with a COBOL compiler. (More about compilers shortly.) *FORTRAN* (an acronym for *For*mula *Tran*slator) is a computer language used primarily for scientific and mathematical purposes. Mathematical symbols and formulas make up the foundation of FORTRAN and enable the programmer to write a complicated mathematics problem with only a few instructions.

Another common language is *BASIC* (an acronym for *B*eginner's *A*ll-purpose *S*ymbolic

*I*nstruction *C*ode). This language was initially developed for use by students, but it has been improved and expanded. Virtually every home computer is equipped for programming in BASIC, and we'll have a good deal more to say about this language later on.

Just as the assembly language is processed through an assembler program, the high-level languages are processed through a program called a *compiler*. It may be convenient to think of assemblers and compilers as being essentially the same thing. The main differences are that the assembler, of course, deals with assembly language and the compiler deals with a high-level language. The most important difference, however, is that, because assembly language is closer to *machine language* (that is, the binary-number language of the computer), the assembler has many fewer steps to reduce the language of the programmer to the language of the machine and is, therefore, a faster program than the compiler. (It is important to bear in mind, however, that when we talk about speed in a computer, we are talking about measurements in *microseconds* [millionths of a second] and even *nanoseconds* [billionths of a second].)

A program that is written in a form that is directly readable by the computer is called an *object program*. A program written in a higher-level language is called a *source program*. The computer translates the source program into an object program before it begins working on the set of instructions.

Most home computers use a special compiler program called an *interpreter*. The compiler converts all the source program's instructions to machine language and then, in effect, steps aside, freeing up memory for other uses. The interpreter, however, converts an instruction, waits for the CPU to implement that instruction, then converts the next instruction, and so on. The interpreter, then, must remain in memory until the entire source program is completed. While this ties up some

of the memory, it is worth the price, because the interpreter permits quick changes in instructions, which the usual kind of compiler does not. With most systems, the sacrifice of memory can be easily compensated for by relatively inexpensive add-on memory. (For technical reasons too complicated and boring to go into here, interpreters work most efficiently with BASIC, less so with more complicated languages.)

BASIC is, beyond question, the most commonly used language for microcomputers. Its appeal is obvious: it is almost identical to English. A raw beginner with a reasonable amount of intelligence can learn to do programming in BASIC with the aid of one or two books and three or four evenings of quiet study and practice.

There are a number of versions of BASIC, including Extended BASIC, BASIC, Tiny BASIC, and Micro BASIC. These vary in versatility and in the cost of the hardware that is required to handle them—Extended BASIC being the most sophisticated, and Micro BASIC the simplest. Differing versions of BASIC exist due to specialized requirements of some systems (for example, color versus black and white) or due to some emphasis or enhancement a software vendor has chosen to add to the minimum standard BASIC. As a result, each manufacturer uses a version of the language that differs somewhat from that of other manufacturers. For that reason, it is impossible to include in this book a course of study in BASIC or even to recommend a course of study. The form of BASIC you learn will depend on the particular machine you own. But these variations should prove to be little more than a minor annoyance; when you have learned BASIC for one machine, you will have little difficulty in learning it for another.

Even within the variations, there are variations. Tiny BASIC, for example, a language originally developed by People's Computer

43

Company, a periodical publisher, enjoyed immediate success and was used for a number of computers before some standardization could be established. (As a result, even Tiny BASIC varies from one computer to another.) The designation "tiny" derives from the fact that one need learn relatively little in order to write programs in the language, and the computer that uses Tiny BASIC is comparatively small, and so is its cost.

Various versions of BASIC are constantly being developed, improved, refined, and dropped. Microcomputer owners who want to know more about BASIC, not only for cultural enhancement but to increase the versatility of their computer use, would do well to subscribe to one of the computer hobby publications or to buy a book devoted exclusively to BASIC.

The microcomputer you buy should come equipped with a manual that includes, among other things, some of the basics of BASIC. It will take a very short time to master the manual. Then a visit to a computer store or a review of publications available by mail will easily and quickly provide you with a more detailed study program for learning the version of BASIC needed for your computer.

7

PROGRAMMING

● What a Program Is

As you now know, probably to the point of boredom, a program is a set of instructions by which a computer performs certain functions or delivers a desired result. The implication is that programming applies only to computers and that it involves very complicated problems and procedures. But as a matter of fact, a program can involve working merely with pencil and paper and solving a fairly simple problem. Indeed, when regarded at its most basic level, a computer is really nothing more than a high-speed, electronic pencil and paper.

Let's consider the kind of problem that you will find in a junior high school student's math book but also the sort that is likely to arise in virtually any household. We'll assume that we have a room that is nine feet by twelve feet and that the room is desperately in need of carpeting. In this morning's newspaper, we have seen an advertisement for exactly the kind of carpeting we need. It is priced at $12.88 per square yard and, this week only, there is a 25 percent reduction on all the carpeting that that particular store is selling. Let's list the data that we have:

1. The room is 9 feet by 12 feet.
2. The carpeting costs $12.88 per square yard.
3. The actual price will be reduced by 25 percent.
4. In our area, we must add a sales tax of 6 percent.
5. There is a delivery charge of $15.

In order to determine the total cost of the carpet, we have to perform the following tasks:

1. We must calculate the total number of square yards needed for our room. (Alternatively, we could break down the price per square yard to a price per square foot, but that would make our job unnecessarily more complicated.)
2. We must calculate the price by multiplying the number of square yards we need by the price per square yard.
3. We must determine the net cost by deducting 25 percent from the total arrived at in Step 2.
4. We must add the sales tax to the result obtained in Step 3.
5. We must add the delivery charge to the total arrived at in Step 4.

If you enjoy wasting time playing with numbers of this sort, you can work out this problem with pencil and paper in a few 'minutes. I prefer to use a simple hand-held calculator that has five functions: addition, subtraction, multiplication, division, and percentage calculation. Calculator in hand, we perform the following steps:

1. We multiply 9 by 12, which gives us 108 square feet.

2. Not unlike a computer, we have stored in our memory the information that there are nine square feet to the square yard, so we divide 108 square feet by 9 to give us 12 square yards.

3. We now multiply the price, $12.88, by 12 for a total price of $154.56.

4. We must now deduct 25 percent of $154.56. There are several ways we can do that, but with our hand-held calculator, all we need to do is key in $154.56, press the MINUS key to show that a subtraction will follow, and then key in the numbers 2 and 5, press the PERCENT key (our readout shows that the deduction will be $38.64), press the EQUAL key, and arrive at a net total of $115.92.

5. The next step is really a reverse of Step 4 and with somewhat different numbers. We key in the result of Step 4, which is $115.92, press the PLUS key to show that an amount is to be added, press the 6 key for the sales tax, press the PERCENT key (the readout shows that $6.9552 is about to be added to the total), press the EQUAL key, and arrive at a total of $122.8752, which is rounded off to $122.88.

6. We now add to $122.88 the delivery charge of $15, and we discover that the total cost of our carpet, delivered, will be $137.88.

In effect, what we have done is, first, written a program and, second, carried it out. To be sure, there are some basic flaws in our example. For one thing, it is very much of an oversimplification. For another, while our "computer" performed many of the tasks necessary in arriving at a result, particularly the most tedious, the most time-consuming, and the ones most subject to error, nevertheless a considerable amount of human participation was involved. If we were dealing with a computer, we would simply inform the machine to perform the following tasks:

1. Calculate square yards.
2. Calculate price for entire room.
3. Deduct discounts.
4. Add sales tax.
5. Add delivery charge.
6. Print out net result.

Of course, the data necessary to perform those calculations would also have to be entered into the machine.

The primary purpose of this overly simple and admittedly less-than-fascinating exercise is to demonstrate what has been stated previously: the computer works only in sequence. Properly programmed, a computer could deliver up that final figure of $137.88 with such speed as to seem instantaneous, but the fact is that a machine can perform only one step at a time, proceeding to each succeeding step in strict accordance with the pattern that has been predetermined by the programmer. A program can be stored in a computer, so the machine can follow the same set of instructions over and over again unless and until those instructions are erased by some other program. This is called *looping,* a process that brings the computer back to the beginning of a set of instructions, ready to repeat them as required.

● Flowcharts

Before beginning a program, you must know three things: (1) You must know what kind of information, or *data,* will be input; (2) you must know what data you want the machine to output; (3) you must know what steps the computer must go through to solve the problem at hand.

The easiest and most efficient way to determine the procedures that you want the computer to follow is to block out those procedures in a diagram. This diagram is called a *flowchart* (also referred to as block diagram, flow diagram, and logic diagram). In effect, the flowchart is a kind of map of the program that is to be written.

On page 48 is an example of a flowchart that has been circulating among computer people for many years. It shows the steps to be taken by the resident breadwinner in getting up and going to work. Designed in the antediluvian days before Women's Liberation, this flowchart makes certain assumptions that today might be considered male-chauvinistic. Nevertheless, sociology aside, it is a good example of what a flowchart looks like. You will note an inset in the upper-right portion of the flowchart; it is a very broad diagram of what has to be done, and it is hardly an adequate one. It is, however, as good a starting point as any, one from which the various refinements can be extrapolated.

The figures shown in the diagram are standard. The rectangle represents the processing step. The diamond shape signifies a decision point. All the symbols used in a flowchart have been standardized; some of the more common ones are shown on page 49. These were drawn with the aid of a *template,* a plastic stencil readily available at computer hobby shops and large commercial stationers'.

● **Using a Flowchart**

A computer, as we said at the outset, does more than compute; it is also capable of making decisions. To be more precise, the user tells the computer what kind of decision she or he wants. The computer then "decides" by making comparisons. Let's consider a specific example and go back to our carpeting problem. Having determined the cost of our carpet earlier in this chapter, we continue leafing through the newspaper, only to discover that this is National Carpet Sales Week and all sorts of carpet retailers are offering all kinds of deals. We now find ourselves confronted with several choices:

1. There is the original offer of carpeting at $12.88 a square yard, less 25 percent discount, plus 6 percent sales tax and a $15 delivery charge.

2. Another store is offering comparable carpeting at $13.10 a square yard. The price includes the sales tax and delivery.

3. A third retailer is offering carpeting at $15 a square yard, with a one-third discount, plus the same 6 percent sales tax and $15 delivery charge.

4. And a fourth retailer is offering carpeting at $20 a square yard, plus a 6 percent sales tax and a $15 delivery charge. This higher-priced carpeting, however, is better-quality and is expected to last about fifteen years, whereas the carpeting being offered by the other three stores is expected to last about ten years.

The question we want our computer to answer is, "Which of the four deals offers the best value?" Which carpet should we buy? With pencil, paper, and patience, the problem is a tedious one, but not a difficult one. We need merely calculate the cost of carpeting for a nine-by-twelve room based on each of the given prices, taking into account the various discounts, the sales tax, and the delivery charge. Once we know that, we divide the net cost of each of the first three offers by ten to give us the cost per square yard per year. We do the same for offer No. 4, except that we divide by fifteen to give us the cost per square yard per year. Faced with this kind of pencil-and-paper computation, the prospect of having a computer do all this dirty work has a cer-

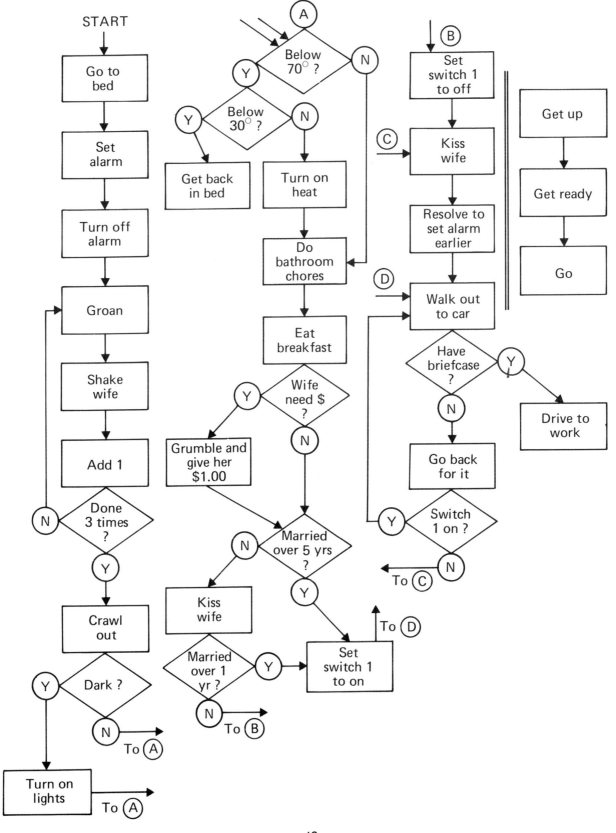

START

Go to bed

Set alarm

Turn off alarm

Groan

Shake wife

Add 1

Done 3 times ? — N / Y

Crawl out

Dark ? — Y / N → To A

Turn on lights — To A

A

Below 70° ? — Y / N

Below 30° ? — Y / N

Get back in bed

Turn on heat

Do bathroom chores

Eat breakfast

Wife need $? — Y / N

Grumble and give her $1.00

Married over 5 yrs ? — N / Y

Kiss wife

Married over 1 yr ? — Y / N → To B

Set switch 1 to on — To D

B

Set switch 1 to off

C

Kiss wife

Resolve to set alarm earlier

D

Walk out to car

Have briefcase ? — Y / N

Drive to work

Go back for it

Switch 1 on ? — Y / N → To C

Get up

Get ready

Go

48

Basic Flowchart Symbols

Input/Output	Process	Flowline	Annotation

Specialized Input/Output Symbols

Punched Card

Magnetic Tape

Punched Tape

Document

Manual Input

Display

Communication
Link

Specialized Process Symbols

Online Storage

Offline Storage

Decision

Predefined Process

Auxiliary Operation

Manual Operation

Additional Symbols

Connector

Terminal

tain undeniable appeal. As a matter of fact, it would probably be a lot easier to work this problem with pencil, paper, and a hand-held calculator, because that would probably take less time than drawing a flowchart and then writing a program. The purpose in using such a simple problem here is merely to show how flowcharting (another one of those strange computerese verbs) is done.

First, we'd set up a data summary, which would look like this:

Room Size: 9 x 12 Feet = 12 Square Yards

CARPET NUMBER	BASIC PRICE PER SQ. YD.	DISCOUNT	SALES TAX	DELIVERY CHARGE	LIFE EXPECTANCY
1	$12.88	25%	6%	$15.00	10 YRS.
2	$13.10	NONE	NONE	NONE	10 YRS.
3	$15.00	1/3	6%	$15.00	10 YRS.
4	$20.00	NONE	6%	$15.00	15 YRS.

Then we would construct the flowchart, which could take several configurations; all of them, however, would look more or less like the chart on the right.

After the above computations have been completed for each carpet, the computer would examine the results to determine which deal offers the best value (i.e., lowest price per square yard per year).

Though we've already established the fact that this problem is of no practical value and will probably take longer to program than to solve with a hand calculator, let's go ahead and write a program for it anyway. (The inherent uselessness of the problem and the time required should not be considered a deterrent. Computer hobbyists are well known for spending ridiculous amounts of time on completely useless projects.)

```
10 INPUT "ENTER ROOM DIMENSIONS
     (FT.)"; W,L
20 A = W × L/9
30 INPUT "ENTER BASIC CARPET PRICE
     PER SQ. YD."; P
```

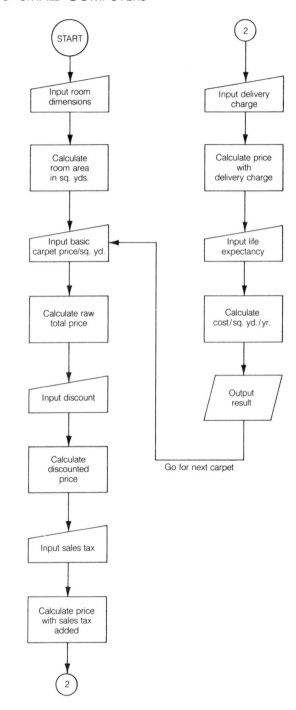

Go for next carpet

```
40 C = P × A
50 INPUT "ENTER DISCOUNT (%)"; D
60 D = D/100
70 C = C − C × D
80 INPUT "ENTER SALES TAX (%)"; T
90 T = T/100
100 C = C + C × T
110 INPUT "ENTER DELIVERY
      CHARGE"; X
120 C = C + X
130 INPUT "ENTER LIFE EXPECTANCY
      OF CARPET"; E
140 C = (C/A)/E
150 PRINT "THE COST OF THIS CARPET
      IS $"; C
160 PRINT "PER SQ. YD. PER YEAR."
170 GOTO 30
180 END
```

There are, as you might imagine, as many ways to write a program as there are programmers, and I would not even suggest that this particular approach is the best one. Here we have created an endless loop by constantly going back for a new basic carpet price (the room dimensions remain the same, so there's no point in entering them for each new price) following each calculation, which means that to get out of the program, we'll have to press a BREAK or ESCAPE key or turn off the computer. "Memory" of the results will have to be a pencil and paper, since there's no provision for retaining each answer, and the "decision" will still have to be made by us based on the pencil-and-paper memory. I could have written the program to retain all the input data and each result, make the comparisons to select the most advantageous price per square yard per year, and report back out all the input data, each calculation, and the final decision, but that truly would have made the solution worse than the problem.

Which isn't the point anyway. The point is,

except for the two steps to convert a percentage to a decimal number, each program step corresponds exactly to one step in the flowchart, and it shouldn't be too difficult for you to see how closely the BASIC program resembles the steps you would take with a hand calculator. And, by the way, actual results from this program were

    $1.14896
     1.31
     1.1903
     1.49667.

● **Software**

The word "software" has been bandied about quite a bit among computerniks. One author, in a textbook for would-be programmers, states unequivocally:

> The software . . . consists of a collection of programs that make the computer easier to use and more effective. This collection of programs, supplied by the manufacturer for extending the capability of the equipment, should be clearly distinguished from *application programs*, written by the *user* of the equipment to get his computational tasks performed. Sometimes the term software is mistakenly used for all aspects of programming.

These days, especially as far as microcomputers are concerned, the ways in which "software" is used effectively negate that last sentence. For our purposes, we may as well go along with the trend and regard all programming as software. (Nonapplication programs are usually known as "system software.")

One of the problems that has confronted the personal computing field for some time has been the unavailability of usable software. The computer operator, therefore, has had to devise his own programs or rely on those developed by hobbyists and published in the various periodicals catering to hobbyists.

On the one hand, this situation has been

ameliorated to the extent that there are now many books available with complete program listings for everything from Gaussian quadrature to Star Trek. These programs are usually written in a general BASIC (unless you find one aimed specifically at your computer) and are easily adapted for a particular system.

On the other hand, there continues to be a problem with software support for new systems. The crabbing about lack of available application programs (and, in this case, lack of peripheral hardware, too) for the recently released IBM Personal Computer attained monumental proportions. It remains a sad fact that when a new computer hits the market, only the manufacturer will have been able to write decent software prior to its release, and the attitude of the manufacturers seems to be to rush to market with the machine with only scant regard for software. It is still a source of bafflement to me how any computer manufacturer can expect you to pay a high price for his fancy new machine and then have it sit there like a great, expensive paperweight until some programs drift along. But that's the way it is. If you are buying a system that is new on the market, make sure that the software you need for your applications is available.

- **Programmable Calculators**

No discussion of programming would be complete without mentioning programmable calculators. A programmable calculator is something less than a computer but certainly something more than an adding machine. Perhaps the primary difference between a programmable calculator and a full-fledged computer is that the calculator, after all, has somewhat limited capabilities. But technological advances, coupled with decreasing manufacturing costs, make the programmable calculator worth considering as an alternative

to the microcomputer, especially for certain business applications. As an executive of one calculator manufacturer commented: "Users of programmable calculators have at their fingertips the equivalent computational capability of a computer that cost about $70,000 in the late 1950s."

Programmable calculators should be considered in situations that involve the performance of repeated operations that are basically the same and where only the data varies. For example, these calculators could be quite useful in working out sales commissions, or converting various specifications to and from the metric system, or calculating compound interest. Most standard calculators are not capable of handling such problems easily, while a computer may be more than is needed.

There are two types of programmable calculators. The preprogrammed calculator has a number of functions that are "hard-wired" into the unit. The program is built into the device. For example, if a company prepares blueprints for submission to a government agency on a regular basis and those blueprints carry specifications given in standard measurements, a preprogrammed calculator could easily convert all of those specifications into the metric system.

Other programmable calculators are capable of accepting specially written programs. Such programs are available in several ways. Not surprisingly, a number of calculator manufacturers offer application software. Where software is not available, the user can, with some models, keep records of the "program" as he keys it into the calculator. On a number of models, however, one need only insert a card or a cartridge into the machine to have the program recorded for repeated use.

Many models of programmable calculators are compatible with a variety of peripherals, such as printers, usually available from the manufacturer. One major manufacturer is al-

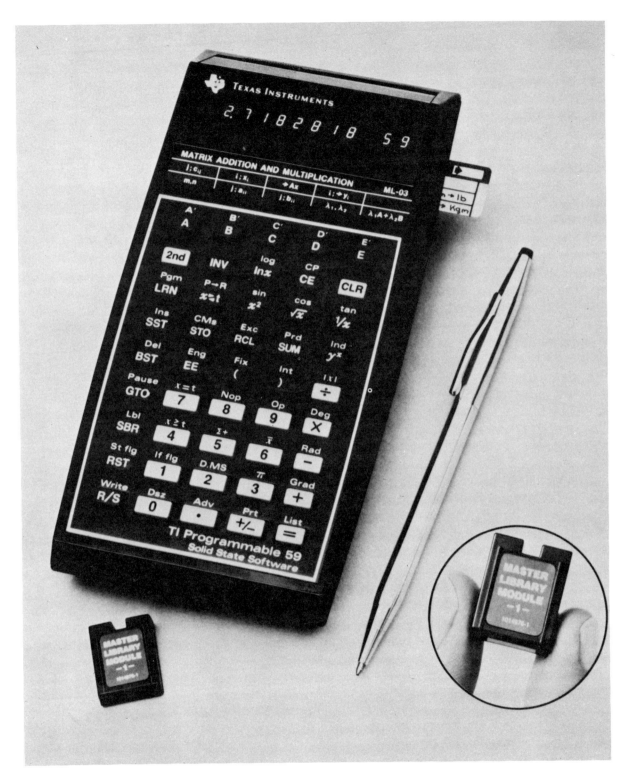

A programmable calculator. The card that has been inserted near the top of the calculator is for a "program" written by the user. The tiny cartridges contain software available for the unit. Courtesy Texas Instruments.

53

ready marketing ROM chips carrying a variety of application programs that need only be plugged into the calculator.

Programmable calculators are available in a broad range of sizes, from those that slip easily into a pocket to those that occupy about the same desk space as a small typewriter.

Prices start at well under a hundred dollars.

Clearly, the microcomputer is no longer merely a hobbyist's diversion with which to play games and indulge in technological mysteries, the solutions to which are shared among a somewhat arcane group.

Microcomputers are ready to go to work.

8

PUTTING YOUR COMPUTER TO WORK

Setting aside for the moment the practical—but admittedly limited—uses of microprocessors in such things as hand-held calculators and household appliances, it must be acknowledged that the real impetus to personal computing came from the computer hobbyist. Now, the dictionary defines a hobby as an "occupation, activity, or interest . . . engaged in primarily for pleasure; a pastime." It was no surprise, therefore, that most hobbyists, when confronted by nonenthusiasts with the question "But what practical use does your home computer have?" responded with a shrug, a sigh, and barely concealed chagrin. Usually, the stammered reply had something to do with the possibilities, potentials, and, almost guiltily, fun and games. In an article written in 1976 for *Science Digest,* I said:

> Claude Kagan, a Western Electric researcher, once suggested to a reporter that by putting physical details—height, weight, age, etc.—of all the people you know into a computer, the computer could then tell whether a stranger was ringing your front doorbell. (Presumably, you could at that point seal up the peephole, which would provide the same information.) Other hobbyists talk of programming home computers to catalog a record collection and balance checkbooks. Also suggested, but apparently never actually tried, is programming a home computer to vacuum the living room or mow the lawn.

That same year, in an article for *Cavalier,* I wrote:

> Almost since the appearance of the first computers, the people involved with them have gotten the machines to play chess and tic-tac-toe, or draw amusing pictures or engage in sophisticated word games. Now, with the advent of the MPU, computer lovers can play these games in their own basements. Still, computer hobbyists are no worse than other hobbyists who love gadgetry for its own sake; not everyone who owns a fancy camera takes good pictures.

Since those articles were written, however, several developments have changed—and are changing—both the attitude toward and the uses of microcomputers, rapidly removing the little marvels from the realm of the fun-loving hobbyist to the domain of the practical householder and/or businessperson.

Price. At a period in our economic history that will live in infamy for its apparently never-ending upward spiral of prices, the electronics industry generally and the microcomputer industry specifically stand out as reversals of this trend. Virtually everything involved in microcomputers, from prepackaged software to the most sophisticated equipment, continues to decline in price. In my *Science Digest* article, I mentioned microcomputer kits retailing for about a thousand dollars on up, which, while not exactly cheap, was certainly far below anybody's conception of what a computer ought to cost. Yet, only eighteen months later, a complete microcomputer, already built and ready to plug in, could be purchased for only six or seven hundred dollars. Technology and production are the underlying reasons for microcomputer prices either holding the line or actually declining. As refinements in the manufacturing processes, as well as in the items being manufactured, continue to increase, the costs of producing them continue to decrease. Furthermore, as more and more people become interested in microcomputers, more and more are sold, and in all but the worst-managed business operations, increased sales invariably lead at least to the potential for lower prices.

Kits and parts. When microcomputers first appeared on the scene, putting them together required the hands of a surgeon and the dedication of a martyr, along with considerable knowledge of and experience with computers and electronics. But increased technology has brought not only lower prices but relative ease of construction and operation. Furthermore, those little pieces of board bristling with wires and pins that are characteristic of microprocessors are now capable of performing many more tasks and functions than their predecessors.

Complete systems. Perhaps the most significant development in the popularization of home computers is the availability of complete systems, not only from computer stores and electronics dealers but from other retailers such as department stores and large mail-order houses. (A number of major retailers have announced plans to begin carrying such products, and if your favorite department store does not have them yet, no doubt it will soon.) The main advantages of these com-plete systems are that they are compact, they require virtually no prior knowledge of electronics or computers, and they require practically no assembly. Obviously, their appearance on the market offers the use of a sophisticated and versatile computer to millions of people who otherwise would not have such access. While these machines are not cheap, they are priced well within the reach of a vast segment of the American population. I have seen, in perfectly ordinary homes, electric typewriters, TV sets, pianos, hi-fi stereo equipment, refrigerators, and many other amenities of contemporary life, each of which costs far more than most of these microcomputers.

Language. The development of high-level computer languages—BASIC, most significantly—makes it possible for the average citizen to communicate with a computer in a language that they can both understand. The appearance and growth of microcomputer magazines, originally intended for the hobbyist, are rapidly expanding the language capabilities not only of computers, but also of the people who own them.

Software. From the very beginning of microprocessing as a hobby, software—or, more accurately, its absence—presented a serious problem. Typically, such software as did exist involved game-playing, and hobbyists who developed their own programs began exchanging them with other hobbyists, either through computer clubs or through the magazines. This practice continues, and as the number of users increases and the degree of sophistication among users increases, no doubt the sharing of software will become a significant aspect of personal computing, as, indeed, it should.

But manufacturers of microcomputers soon realized that if they were to expand the market for their equipment, they would also have to expand the capability of a greater number of consumers to use that equipment. The result is that a considerable amount of software is now being made available by the companies that make the computers. This is not particularly innovative; the corporate giants who manufacture huge computers have always supplied software to their customers. So have companies set up specifically for the purpose of developing and marketing software. These practices have now filtered down to the microcomputer industry, so that manufacturers, software companies, and users are all making software available to the microcomputer user.

As a direct result of these newer, smarter, and easier-to-operate computers, much of life's tedium can be relegated to a machine. To be sure, there are limitations to the type and especially to the size of a task that a microcomputer can be expected to perform. A computer has only so much memory and there is a limit as to how much memory can be added on even if that limit ultimately is determined by financial, rather than technological, considerations. Furthermore, a microcomputer can do many of the things that a large computer can, but certainly not all of them— at least not nearly as fast. If you operate a business that employs fifty or sixty people, you can probably set up a payroll program that can be conveniently run on a microcomputer. But if you are responsible for the payroll for two or three thousand people, by the time your microcomputer finishes the run, most of your employees will be ready for retirement.

There are really two kinds of limitations on the various tasks a microcomputer can perform: (1) the limitations of the computer itself, and (2) the limitations of your own imagination and creativity in developing programs that use your microcomputer to its maximum capacity. The computer applications that follow, therefore, should be regarded merely as suggestions for possible use

and should not be regarded as restrictions on the versatility of microcomputers.

● Record Keeping

This is a general, broad, all-purpose category that is likely to mean all things to all people. For a physician, for example, record keeping with a microcomputer means that he can maintain all of his patients' records in a safe, convenient, compact location: the computer system. For the phonograph-record collector, setting up a filing system by using the computer is a task of the utmost simplicity. The same is true for someone with a large personal library. One need only assign each new acquisition a number, in sequence. In other words, if the last book or record you acquired is numbered 142, then the next one you acquire will be numbered 143. Using those numbers as a basis, you can then input enough information to keep a handy, accurate file. Cross-referencing becomes a simple matter. The book collector can enter the data under author, title of book, subject matter of book, name of illustrator, and any other details that could prove useful, including—if the collector buys, sells, and trades rare volumes —the purchase price and date of purchase. The record collector, following the same general idea, could cross-reference each new entry by composer, performer, type of music, type of instrumental solo, and any other pertinent information. As for the physician, with a modicum of programming, he or she can easily cross-reference patients according to type of illness, sex, age, socioeconomic level, etc., so that at a moment's notice he or she could extract interesting, useful, and perhaps even vital information about the state of a community's health.

Microcomputer owners who belong to organizations could suddenly become very popular by offering to maintain any number of records for that organization. Membership rolls, financial records, and other types of files could be stored for ready retrieval by your microcomputer. In fact, the storage media dedicated to such record keeping might even provide a tax deduction if the organization is charitable or not-for-profit. (It is always advisable to consult an accountant about such things; I will not accompany you to the IRS office.)

Perhaps the most useful application of microcomputers for purposes of record keeping is that of personal finances. I predict that in the near future, perhaps even by the time this book appears in print, you will be able to buy software that will enable you to maintain clear and accurate financial records at home. But even if that prediction should fail to materialize, it is still possible, with relative ease, to involve a microcomputer in financial planning for the family.

You could begin by inputting a rough budget: anticipated annual income, known expenses for the year (rent or mortgage, heating costs, approximate utility costs —based on the previous year's costs—insurance, tuition, etc.). You would then add the amount you are prepared to allow for so-called discretionary expenditures such as entertainment, vacation, etc. The program should include some predetermined rules for dealing with unexpected expenses. For example, if automobile maintenance or heating bills exceed a given monthly limit, then entertainment or vacation costs are to be reduced by whatever amount is decided upon.

When a bill comes in, the amount of the bill and the category to which it applies are keyed into the computer so that a comparison can be made between the planned expenses and the actual expenses. In this way, with the help of the computer, you could keep a continual watch on your budget, adjusting as necessary. (According to one report, there should now be on the market a program for bill juggling.)

Another form of financial record keeping is the relatively simple process of checking one's bank balance. If you find yourself writing out some twenty-five to thirty checks each month, even if you are proficient with numbers and own a good calculator, it probably takes you at least fifteen minutes to check out the balance in your checkbook against the monthly statement you receive from the bank. With a microcomputer, this could be handled as an ongoing process. Every few days, you would simply key in the amounts of the checks you have written. Your program would provide for flagging those checks that have not yet cleared the bank at the time the statement arrives. Once the program has been designed and is running, you could probably check your bank balance in a minute or two, if not in a matter of seconds.

It seems almost too obvious to mention that one of the best applications of a microcomputer for record keeping is in the operation of a small business. A microprocessor is ideal for inventory control, payroll, accounts receivable, accounts payable, interest rates, mortgage rates, amortization, and a host of other records and data that are tedious and annoying when they have to be accumulated for any reason—usually for tax purposes—but which become much less so when the data, a bit at a time, is input to the computer and can be recalled literally with the touch of a button or two.

● **Investment Portfolios**

Many years ago, I served time as a mutual-fund salesman and learned a little about stocks and bonds (most of which, mercifully, I have forgotten). There were many "systems" for making market predictions, ranging from sunspot cycles to an intricate formula of economic trends and factors such as the prime interest rate, the price of gold, gross national product, etc. The one that stands out most in my mind was a system that claimed that the movement of the market would follow that of the hemlines of women's skirts by approximately six months; that is, if skirts rose, approximately six months later the market would rise. If they fell, the market would do likewise. This method was remarkable not so much for its attractiveness as a means of keeping track of the stock market but because it was surprisingly accurate. Unfortunately, recent fashion trends and sociological changes in attitudes toward conformity have made this technique inoperable. I maintain, however, that it is about as sensible and accurate an approach to market predictability as any other, including one that involves careful tracking and analysis of such things as the Dow-Jones averages with a computer. At one time, particularly in the early days of computers, people who had access to computers spent a lot of time playing around with stock market predictions. For some reason, such activity seems to have diminished greatly—at least, it is no longer discussed very much. That may be because even a computer, however sophisticated, is incapable of dealing with the frivolities of the investment markets or because those who have failed have simply given up and stopped talking about it, while those who have succeeded prefer to keep their secret to themselves. If you are obsessed with the idea of computerizing a system for winning at stocks and bonds—or, for that matter, any other form of gambling, such as blackjack or horse racing—then, by all means, put your computer to good use. You may actually hit upon one of those well-kept secrets. Even if such secrets do not actually exist, you should not be deterred by the failure of others. After all, Thomas Edison and Albert Einstein persisted in areas where others failed. And patent attorneys are constantly turning away would-be clients who are convinced that they have invented the true perpetual motion machine.

Perhaps a discussion of computerized stock market predictions properly belongs in Chapter 10, "Fun and Games," but quite seriously, it is not a possibility that should be lightly tossed aside. After all, stock market behavior is at least somewhat cyclical and such cycles do seem to occur with some regularity. I remember, as a mutual-fund salesman, being taken on a tour of the offices of what was then a relatively new and very hot mutual fund, managed by a company headed by a young man who was then affectionately referred to as "the *Wunderkind* of Wall Street." The young president's office had two walls covered, from ceiling to floor, with a chart showing the New York *Times* stock averages for a great many years (I cannot remember the exact time period covered). Only occasionally was there an erratic dip or unexpected high. It was easy to see, by looking at the chart, how the market moves not in volcanic eruptions or lead-weight descents, but, rather, in a fairly smooth-flowing, wavelike pattern of ups and downs. Certainly, it can do no harm to place so-called "mind bets" in certain specific investments (e.g., the stocks of a particular company, or the bonds of a particular municipality, or certain specific commodities), industries (aerospace, electronics, entertainment and leisure, etc.), or in trading areas (stock exchanges, commodity exchanges, over-the-counter). If you see some sort of trend emerging, one that continues over an extended period of time and appears to offer the possibilities of predictability, you could follow that trend to see whether you have, in fact, hit upon a winning system, at which point you could risk some hard cash. (I want it clearly understood, however, that none of the foregoing is to be construed as a recommendation or endorsement on my part. I have no idea whether the electronics and aerospace industries are worthy investments now or later. Proceed at your own risk.)

Of course, there is much more to the possibilities of a working relationship between investments and microcomputers. Certainly, a home computer offers one of the best ways to keep track of your investment portfolio, particularly when you remember that "investment portfolio" covers stocks, bonds, mutual-fund holdings, mortgages (the kind in which someone pays you, not the other way around), United States Savings Bonds, savings accounts at savings banks and savings-and-loan associations, and life insurance policies, particularly those that pay dividends and/or annuities. If you are holding, for example, so-called "blue chip" or "gilt edge" stocks, happily collecting quarterly dividends, you may not realize that given the current rate of inflation, your money might earn more for you if you sold those stocks at the current market rate and reinvested the proceeds from that sale in something yielding a higher rate. If you are socking away funds in a savings account against some future goal, such as retirement or college tuition, you may be surprised to learn that the inflation rate, your tax bracket, and the rate of interest you receive for your savings all combine to gradually chip away at a sensible retirement or tuition fund. Perhaps that money would serve you better in municipal bonds, which, while paying a lower interest rate, are nontaxable and may, therefore, provide greater earnings for you. A microcomputer can be an extremely handy method of keeping track of the entire portfolio, the purchase price of each item in that portfolio, the interest or dividends each item yields, and the current market value of each investment. As simple a technique as dollar cost averaging can be made even more simple with the help of a home computer. (Dollar cost averaging, as the term suggests, involves averaging out the cost of a particular investment by investing a fixed amount of money in the same stock at regular intervals. Your money buys more shares when the market is low and fewer shares when the market is high, but the average *cost* per share is lower than the average *price* per share. Yes, I know, this is a book about computers and not about investments.)

Bearing in mind that a computer can perform calculations, make comparisons, and then make decisions based on those comparisons, a microcomputer would seem to be an eminently sensible method of keeping track of an investment.

• Mailing Lists

On any typical day, you are likely to receive a letter or statement from your bank, a catalog from a mail-order firm, an offer from a magazine inviting you to subscribe, and many other pieces of mail designed, in one way or another, to separate you from a portion of your money. In almost every case, that mail has been addressed by a computer. Commercial mailing lists are usually maintained by a computer in accordance with various categories. Geography, income level, size and type of home, political-party affiliation, marital status, number and/or ages of children, occupation or profession—all these and others are logical types of mailing lists for various businesses to maintain. In fact, the reason you often receive several copies of the same piece of mail is that you are on more than one mailing list. (In our house, one of the more pleasant diversions that the daily mail brings is seeing how many ways the name "Grosswirth" can be spelled.) The application of similar techniques can be most helpful in maintaining a personal mailing list and is easy to arrange with a microcomputer.

It is perhaps a little silly and pretentious to go to a computer to find out Aunt Harriet's address when you want to send her a birthday card, when all you have to do is flip to the proper section of the address book that you keep near the telephone. But suppose the month of December is drawing near and you find that, as usual, you will be sending greeting cards to perhaps a hundred or more people. Some of those people will be receiving Christmas cards while others will probably expect Hanukkah cards. Going through that address book a name at a time to determine who gets what kind of card can make a serious dent in the holiday spirit, whereas punching a couple of buttons on your microcomputer can separate the Jews from the Christians in no time, for once a not-unworthy process.

Now that you have the list separated, you and your spouse will certainly go over it, a name at a time, to determine whether "they" sent "us" a card last year. By keying in the names of people you want to send cards to and those you have received cards from, at the appropriate time you could have your microcomputer print out address labels for those people from whom you received cards last year, labels for the people to whom you will send cards regardless of whether they sent any last year, and a list of the people about whom a decision has to be made. There are those who will argue that computerizing a holiday-card mailing list and printing out the names and addresses make the process of sending such cards cold, impersonal, and commercial-looking. My reply to such arguments is that the mailing of holiday cards *en masse* with the name of the sender already imprinted on the inside of the card is already cold, impersonal, and commercial—to such an extent that making life a little simpler by using a personal computer will do little, if anything, to make matters worse.

I am at a loss to understand why what little literature there is in the personal computer field has failed to point out the value of a microcomputer for maintaining a mailing list beyond the Christmas-card application. It seems to me to be an eminently useful occupation to separate one's personal mailing list into certain categories: husband's relatives, wife's relatives, husband's friends, wife's friends, mutual friends, children's friends, business associates, etc. Surely everyone has had or will have a situation in which one or more of these categories must be separated from the entire mailing list. Invitations to a party or a wedding, people who have to be called in case of an emergency or a death in the family, people to whom social announcements must be sent—how much easier to key all of this data into storage once and have it available for almost instant use whenever it is needed.

- **A Computerized Kitchen**

It has actually been suggested that the owner of a microcomputer take a complete inventory of the family larder, key the quantities into the computer, and, every time an item is used, key that in too, so that the computer can alert the dedicated and efficient homemaker when supplies are running low. In my opinion, utilizing the computer for such purposes is sheer nonsense. Just imagine telling your computer that you have a dozen frankfurters in the refrigerator and then, three days later, when you want a quick lunch, running over to the machine to let it know that you are about to consume two of those frankfurters and a can of baked beans. In my house, such a system would break down in a matter of days, if not hours. There are, however, some very practical and time-saving applications of the microcomputer to the kitchen, not the least of which is, in fact, an inventory—not an inventory of the contents of the refrigerator or the cupboard over the sink, but an inventory of long-term supplies.

Many families long ago recognized the value of owning a deep freezer, which sits in the basement and accommodates large quantities of meat and other frozen foods, purchased in quantity when prices are low and used as needed. Certainly, an inventory of such supplies can be kept by a microcomputer. An inventory of this type serves two purposes: first, of course, it lets you know when you are running low on some item. Second, it lets you know, should there be a particularly good value available, whether you have room for the product you want to purchase. Obviously, this method need not apply only to frozen food. If you have the storage space for canned goods, laundry products, paper goods, and other nonperishables, it makes sense to buy in quantity when such items are on sale. In many communities, there are wholesale markets that sell at close-to-wholesale prices to consumers willing to buy in case lots and cart the stuff home in their own cars.

Another useful application of the microcomputer to the kitchen is in the filing of recipes. Dedicated cooks often have efficient and elaborate (although the two terms are not necessarily synonymous) recipe files, consisting of file-card boxes, scrapbooks, notebooks, and albums, filled with recipes clipped from newspapers and magazines, and a quantity of recipes stored inside the chef's brain, destined to die when the cook does. One of the very first practical applications of a microcomputer is the computerization of all those recipes. Consider, for a moment, just a few of the possibilities. Based upon how the data is entered, a microcomputer could yield up in a trice all the available recipes for chocolate desserts. In the event of a less-than-abundantly stocked pantry, an occurrence that usually coincides with the arrival of unexpected guests, a mere touch at the computer terminal can deliver all the recipes available that include one common ingredient—say, tuna fish. The home computer can be used to plan menus. "I have a chicken," the cook says to the computer. "What goes well with chicken?" The computer answers immediately, in accordance with the cook's tastes. Thus, if the user believes that succotash and spinach go well with chicken, the computer will remind him or her that this

is a preferred combination (although not one that is preferred by me). Spend a couple of hours with your input terminal in one hand and a good calorie chart in the other, and, forever after, the computer can give you the total calorie count of a planned meal. For people on special diets, the computer can store the nutritive composition of foods so that you know immediately what to feed Uncle Herman, who is coming to dinner tonight and is on a low-sodium regimen.

The other night, I decided to take a brief respite from the creative effort that is this book and try out a new and relatively simple recipe for cookies. The recipe calls for three eggs. To my dismay, I discovered that there was only one egg in the refrigerator. Attempting to divide the remainder of the ingredients by one third was more trouble than I was willing to invest in the project, so I turned instead to the self-hypnosis of television. Had I but properly programmed a microcomputer, it could easily have told me what one third of all of the other ingredients in that cookie recipe would be.

The uses of a microcomputer for someone who spends a great deal of time in the kitchen seem almost infinite. Conversion of weights and measures, decreasing or expanding recipes, menu planning, calorie counting, keeping track of cooking times, keeping track of people's favorite foods or food restrictions, and making price comparisons are some of the applications I can think of. No doubt, you can think of a great many more.

• A Computerized Environment

If you have a thermostat, it will turn on the furnace (or the air-conditioner) when the temperature of the area in which the thermostat is situated differs from the one set on the thermostat. It will do that regardless of whether the room is occupied, about to be occupied, or just recently vacated. But if a computer is programmed with the general habits of the members of the household and if it is equipped with the necessary sensors, it could turn heating and cooling devices on and off in a pattern that is compatible with the goings and comings of the family. It could also perform such functions as turning on washing machines or dishwashers at those times of day when the electricity rate is lower. One rather sophisticated application is the controlling of a lawn sprinkler. Sensors placed in the soil could measure the amount of moisture and feed that data to the computer, which would then determine if more moisture is required. If so, it turns on the sprinkler. Other sensors measure the amount of sunlight to make sure that the sprinkling is not done at a time when the sun is in a position to damage the foliage.

An extremely valuable application of a microcomputer would be that of giving a home a lived-in look when the occupants are away. The computer could be programmed to turn lights on and off at random and cause the radio or TV set to play during hours when people would normally be home.

By now, you have probably realized that almost all of the applications mentioned in environmental control can be accomplished without a computer; thermostats, timers, photoelectric cells, and moderately priced security devices can be purchased to achieve these very same effects. Certainly, that makes sense and it would be extravagant to purchase a microcomputer just for these purposes. Furthermore, to program a computer to perform such tasks requires a considerable amount of knowledge and experience as well as the expense of the admittedly unique "peripherals" that would be required to achieve these ends. Again, no argument. The point to remember, however, is that a microcomputer is a multipurpose device. It would probably be pointless to buy one for the control of one's home environment, but if you are going to buy one anyway for other reasons, it would be just as extravagant to avoid at least a consideration of this kind of application for the machine.

Such applications tend to conjure up images of the science fiction movie in which an obedient and tireless robot serves breakfast in bed, washes the dishes, and sees the children safely off to school. As farfetched and remote as such images seem to be, they are not beyond the realm of possibility or practicality. After all, millions of Americans are awakened to the sound of gentle music. If they fail to respond, the sound gets louder and gradually harsher, changing from music to a chime to a loud buzzer. At the same time, their coffee automatically starts perking, their bath water starts heating up in the boiler in the basement, and warm air is flowing through the heat registers in the bedroom. Had you suggested at the beginning of this century that any of this was possible, you would have been laughed out of town.

• **Programmed Learning**

Programmed learning is a method of teaching that involves a carefully structured presentation of the information to be learned. In this method, the learning process begins with the simplest and most readily understood information and gradually increases in difficulty and complexity. Along the way, there are stages, built into the program, at which the learner tests himself.

There are a number of advantages to programmed learning. First, it permits the learner to proceed at his own pace. Second, it enables him to absorb the information one step at a time. Third, it permits him to determine, as he proceeds, whether he is, in fact, learning. If he is not, there are usually drills and techniques built into the program for reinforcing the learning process.

Lots of programmed learning materials

exist in book form, but there are also devices known as "teaching machines." These can be highly sophisticated and very elegant electronic setups, but almost everyone has seen a much simpler version, usually available in most toy departments. In this version, the teaching machine consists of a box with a series of little windows or slides. A problem— say, a multiplication problem—is presented. The user offers a solution to the problem and can then see, by exposing another window, whether he has gotten the right answer. In some versions of this machine, the user cannot proceed to the next question until he corrects his answer to the current question.

Of all the tasks for which a microcomputer is suited, probably none can be handled more effectively than programmed learning. The presence of children of school or preschool age in a household should be a strong inducement for owning a home computer. Already, programmed learning software exists. One manufacturer of a complete, ready-to-plug-in computer system offers at a very low price software for learning math. Additional software from a variety of sources is available. More is certainly on the way.

What is perhaps more interesting, however, is the fact that anyone who owns a microcomputer and knows how to program it can purchase programmed learning materials in book form and, using fairly simple programming skills, write a computer program and turn his microcomputer into a highly efficient teaching machine.

(If any of the foregoing is a little confusing, reread it, keeping in mind that the word "programmed" is, perforce, being used in two ways. In one instance, it refers to the programming that is done for your computer. In other instances, it is used to describe a particular form of learning material, which may or may not be computerized; computerization has nothing to do with "programmed learn-ing," as that phrase is defined. Is that clear now?)

• Word Processing

Word processing as a computer concept has its origins in the giant corporations, but its appeal to those involved in personal computers is undeniable. Essentially, word processing involves the following basic concepts:

First, you compose whatever it is you are going to compose—a letter, a manuscript, advertising copy, a sales, technical, or instruction manual, etc.—on an input device that displays. That can be a typewriter, a CRT (cathode-ray-tube terminal, the video-screen type of I/O device), or a teletypewriter. You can then edit, making corrections, deletions, changes, and additions on the same input device. Everything goes into the computer and, when you are finished and press the right button, the computer prints out a perfect copy, free of errors, and set up in any way you specify. It can be single-spaced, double-spaced, justified right and left, with alternate paragraphs indented—just about any kind of layout you can imagine.

Since you have reached this far in this book, you probably don't need this admonition, but I will include it anyway: The computer does not make typing mistakes. But neither can it correct bad spelling, faulty grammar, or improper punctuation that is fed to it by the operator. (Unless, of course, it has been preprogrammed to correct such errors, a nicety not yet available for most microcomputers. Indeed, many large computers are ill-equipped to handle some of these problems. Most major newspapers are prepared by word-processing systems, a fact easily detectable by the annoying and often ludicrous ways in which words are sometimes hyphenated at the end of a line.)

In its simplest form, a word-processing system makes the additions, deletions, or changes just mentioned. Ideally, however, a good word-processing system should also be able to move sections of copy around. There are word-processing routines that can seek out every occurrence of a single word or phrase in the text, remove it, and insert another word or phrase. It is possible to have this desirable feature in a microcomputer system, provided there is enough memory.

It has been suggested that one practical use of a word-processing system is the production of those abominable Christmas letters that some people delight in sending. By breaking down the information that would go into such a letter, it would then be possible to select those pieces of information that a given recipient or group of recipients would be most interested in receiving. Then, while reviewing the mailing list, one could single out either the specific topics or the individual paragraphs that would be most likely to intrigue the individual on the list. The computer, having no sense of taste or decency, would then type the letter as instructed. The computerized letter could even be "personalized" by inserting the recipient's name at various places in the letter.

A far more worthwhile use of a word-processing routine is a variation on that theme. A system could easily be set up for a charitable organization, a religious group, or a school, selecting information or paragraphs that might be of specific interest to the recipient. For example, a school with classes ranging from kindergarten through eighth grade could send out letters in which the opening paragraphs would make reference to the grade level relevant to the recipient's child. A religious congregation could similarly feature, in the opening paragraphs, the timing and convenience of religious services, religious-school facilities for children and adults, and activities for single people, young people, married people, old people, etc.

For a sensible word-processing system, you will probably need a microcomputer with at least 16K of memory. That, however, is minimal; 32K should be considered for a more complete system.

Also needed is some kind of mass data storage. For the most part, word-processing routines are sequential and are therefore highly adaptable to tape cassettes for storage. But if speed is important, floppy-disk storage is advised.

If you decide to use your microcomputer for word processing, investigate the possibilities and availability of a word-processing program written in machine language. You will remember that a microcomputer must "translate" the high-level language to machine language and that this requires more memory than if the program were written in machine language directly. Now you are adding a program for word processing, taking up still more memory. In other words, first the program that changes the high-level language into machine language must be loaded into the computer. Then the word-processing program itself must be loaded. Finally, the copy that is to be processed is input. The need for memory with a substantial capacity becomes obvious. If, however, you can use a word-processing program that is written in machine language, you are, in effect, freeing up a good portion of the memory for use on the text to be edited.

• Business Applications

So far, in discussing the various ways of putting a microcomputer to work, we have, for the most part, confined ourselves to uses within a home setting. In doing so, we have, willy-nilly, crisscrossed the line between personal use and business use. But when it comes to business applications that require such data as detailed daily inventories, up-to-date accounts receivable, expenses, posting to various bookkeeping accounts, sales and production data, etc., we are beginning to move away somewhat from the relatively low cost of microcomputers.

For one thing, it is recommended that a microcomputer for use in a small business should have a minimum of 32K memory; the more memory, the costlier the system. It is also recommended that disks be used for memory and storage; disks cost more than tape cassettes. In most instances, a video-type terminal will probably be needed for keeping track of input and output, but some method of obtaining *hard copy* (printed sheets) will also be necessary. In addition, mass storage should be provided for.

Another important consideration in using a microcomputer for general business applications is the effect on the business that a possible breakdown might have. Computers, alas, do occasionally break down. That could mean anywhere from several hours to several days without the use of the computer, depending upon one's own ability to make repairs and the availability of parts and service. An important consideration, therefore, before using a microcomputer to run a small business, is whether that business can function when the computer does not. Before entrusting your business to a computer, make sure that the following conditions exist:

1. The computer itself is a well-constructed model that has been tested through use and comes from a known, reliable manufacturer.

2. Application programs for the computer are readily available. It may be necessary to revise existing application programs some-

what; this can often be done with a minimum of difficulty.

3. The computer has a sufficient amount of memory to retain not only anticipated requirements, but a bit more in the event of unanticipated needs.

4. The computer has sufficient versatility to expand its capacity, both for memory and for peripherals.

5. It has a reliable disk-operating system.

6. Software, with sufficient flexibility to adapt to changing business conditions, is available.

7. A printer that will provide printouts of programs and reports is, or can be, included in the system.

8. There is an adequate data-backup provision, a means of storing programs and data for possible future use.

9. Adequate servicing of the equipment is available.

Upon reviewing the above checklist, it becomes apparent that microcomputers for business use are somewhat more complex and expensive than they are for home use. They are not, however, beyond the means of many small businesses. And they are, of course, a legitimate business expense. If you own and operate a small business, and the details and paperwork are beginning to get you down, you might want to have a long and serious discussion with your accountant about having a computer of your very own.

Once you do have one, it can help you escape from the pressures and trials of the everyday world. Those little electronic devils just love to play games with people.

9

MICROCOMPUTERS IN BUSINESS

by Richard Amyx

● **Home Computer / Small Computer**

There are now at least a hundred kinds of home computers, personal computers, and "small" computers on the market. Some, which feature in their advertisements such things as fancy graphics and lifelike games that can be just plugged in and run, appear to be aimed at one market. Others, which feature programs such as home finances and educational aids (usually in addition to a number of games) and suggest that more hardware and peripherals can be added on, seem to be aimed at another. Still another group may have only an occasional television ad or restrain itself to dignified, reserved magazine advertisements (and in either case say nothing about games but emphasize such features as ease of use, dependability, and reliability). Which of these is a "home" computer, which is a "personal" computer, and which is a "small" computer?

I honestly don't know. My own system, which began as the basic six-hundred-dollar TRS-80 Level I, 4K starter unit that appeared on the market in 1978, was originally purchased as an item of entertainment and hobby interest. It now has 48K memory, two diskette drives, a printer, and an acoustic *modem* connected to it (a modem is a device to convert the serial-computer information to audible tones that can be transmitted over the telephone lines), and sees about 80 percent of its use as a word processor, 10 percent in other business or quasi-business uses, and the remaining 10 percent in entertainment. A friend who owns a Wang minicomputer (admittedly a big step above the microcomputer systems we're discussing in this book) strictly for business still gets a kick out of playing Pac-Man on it. The recently released IBM microcomputer, which for all the world seems to me to be a "small" computer intended for serious use in the business world, calls itself the "IBM *Personal* Computer." A book published by the Texas Instruments Learning Center shows pictures of two microcomputer systems that are, as far as I'm concerned, functional equivalents. Yet one is identified as a "home" computer and the other is identified as a "personal" computer. The accompanying text doesn't offer any suggestions as to how the distinction was made.

I propose, as a tentative working definition,

the notion that at one end of the scale there is a group of microcomputers that doesn't seem to offer much more than games and a few of the "home finance" type of programs, and at the other end of the scale is a set that offers no games at all but presents its constituents as reliable tools for use in serious applications. In between is a wide range that incorporates some of the features of each.

I think the way out of the "home-personal-small" dilemma is to look at the *similarities* among the microcomputer systems, rather than their differences. The majority of microsystems available today share these characteristics:

• They are controlled by an eight-bit microprocessor, usually the Zilog Z80 or Z80-A, the Motorola 6502, or the Intel 8085.

• They offer as part of the system or as an optional add-on, RAM up to 32K, 48K, or 64K.

• They offer as part of the system or as optional add-ons fast magnetic media, either floppy diskette or hard disk.

• They offer as part of the system or as optional add-ons interfaces for printers of one kind or another.

• They offer as part of the system or as an optional add-on RS-232 capability (telephone communications).

If any system you're looking at has these characteristics, then it will probably be applicable to small-business uses. On the other hand, if a system that's caught your eye *doesn't* have these characteristics, then you'd probably be disappointed. For business uses, you would want the maximum RAM the processor is capable of handling. RAM is where all the real work of a microsystem is done, and having a limited amount will either limit your capabilities or make much of the work tedious. You will need fast media

(floppy diskette or hard disk) for both its capacity and its speed. Cassettes are too slow for real-world computer work. If you intend to use your computer for business, you will need a printer of some kind—creating printed reports from stored data is a large part of most business applications. Telephone communication is optional, but chances are good that you will find a use for it. The cost of including an RS-232 interface is minimal compared to the total cost of any system. All these characteristics, the need for them, and their uses are discussed in greater detail below.

Otherwise, forget about whether a microcomputer system might be a home computer, a personal computer, or a small computer, and just consider it to be a microcomputer system. What it will do, not what it's called, is what's important.

When to Buy

If you already own a microcomputer, that's one thing. But if being able to use one for business is affecting your decision whether or not to buy, then there are several factors to take into consideration. While a microcomputer is a powerful tool and can be a very helpful business ally, you should be sure that what you buy will do what you want it to do.

A pickup is a truck, and has more carrying capacity than a family sedan does, but a pickup is not a diesel-powered tractor-and-trailer rig. It has uses for which it is ideally suited, but it will haul big loads only small pieces at a time. If you need the carrying capacity of a pickup only occasionally, then it doesn't make economic sense to buy one. In the same way, a microcomputer has more calculating power than a hand calculator does, but it is not a mainframe system like the computers normally associated with big business. A microcomputer has uses for which it is ideally suited, but it will perform large tasks only in small pieces. If you need the calculating power of a computer only occasionally, then it wouldn't make economic sense to buy one.

One of the computer applications commonly associated with business is accounting, and the temptation is always there to have a machine that will flawlessly perform arithmetic and otherwise take care of much of the drudgery that bookkeeping involves. For a small company, purchasing a microcomputer as an accounting tool must be cost-effective; a large company would have record-keeping needs beyond what could reasonably be expected of a microcomputer.

A starter microcomputer system suitable for small business will cost between twenty-five hundred and five thousand dollars. If the company is small—on the order of, say, four employees—then it might not pay to buy the computer. The computer *should* be able to save one existing employee enough time that a new one won't have to be hired. If you were to spend the cash to buy a computer and then still have to hire another employee, then the decision to buy might not be a wise one. Remember too that a microcomputer purchased for accounting can also be put to other uses: word processing, inventory keeping, scheduling, modeling. If you intend to use the microcomputer for one purpose only, allowing it to sit idle most of the time, then you may not really be ready for one.

On the other hand, if you employ a hundred or more employees, then probably your needs exceed the capacity of a microcomputer system. You could find a system that *would* do what you wanted, but you'd have to be prepared to allow a week to get some particular job done. Some systems advertise an unbelievable amount of "memory" capacity, and unbelievable is just the word to describe the claim. In a microcomputer, "memory" usually refers to RAM. There is, however, a technique called *virtual memory,* which uses disk

or diskette in a way that makes the computer appear to have much more memory than its inherent addressing capability would permit. The technique is useful, but slow. Access time to RAM is about two hundred nanoseconds; access time to a diskette is on the order of six milliseconds. Although these times mean virtually nothing in the macroworld, recall that while a nanosecond is a billionth of a second, a millisecond is a thousandth of a second. This means that six milliseconds is thirty thousand times as long as two hundred nanoseconds, and a factor of thirty thousand is significant when you consider performing an operation thousands of times. I have seen advertised several mailing-label programs that feature a sort-merge (another technique for alphabetizing or zip-code sorting more items than RAM will hold) capable of dealing with ten thousand names and addresses. I don't doubt that these programs work, but I would expect them to take eight hours or more to carry out such a large sort-merge.

The bottom line to all this is, Don't be fooled by numbers. If a salesman tells you that his computer has "memory" capacity much greater than similar machines, ask him what it really means. Is it RAM or virtual memory? If some system claims to handle very large amounts of data, ask what it means in real-world terms. How long will the operation take? Will the machine carry out the process untended, or will an operator have to change diskettes several times along the way? Yes, the machine may indeed leap tall buildings at a single bound—but will it take a week to do it? Find out *first* what the specifics will mean to you in terms you can understand. Learning these things *after* you've plunked down your money can make you unhappy.

Who'll Be the Expert?

Nearly every microcomputer system on the

market advertises with phrases such as "easy to use," "no computer or programming experience necessary," "user-friendly," "completely menu-driven," or "highly interactive." These claims are probably true: a good program should be both understandable and usable by a person without skills remarkably beyond those normally associated with routine office work. But it is unrealistic to expect to get maximum use out of a microcomputer without having some knowledge of how it works, its capabilities, and its limitations. And it is a maxim in the field that if it is in any way possible to misinterpret an instruction, then the instruction will be misinterpreted.

One computer company featured an accounting system that was advertised to be foolproof, yet a client firm complained time and again that they were getting data scrambled. The programmer who wrote the system talked to the client on the telephone more than once, and each time went through the data entry process step by step, and each time confirmed that the operator was doing exactly what she was supposed to. Finally he went and visited the company and instructed the operator: "Now, Myra, I'm going to stand here behind you and watch you enter data. Please enter the data exactly as you always do, and don't leave out any steps." Myra, who was good at repetitive chores such as data entry, went through the steps flawlessly, and when she got the screen message indicating that all data had been entered, turned the terminal off.

The flabbergasted programmer asked Myra why she had turned off the terminal. She explained: "When I finish entering data, the computer tells me, 'I'm processing the data now. Please do not disturb me.' I thought the best way to keep it from being disturbed was just to turn the terminal off." Thus was the programmer hoist with his own user-friendliness.

A typist is expected to be able to correct mistakes, change a ribbon, know about some of the idiosyncrasies of the typewriter, and perform minor maintenance operations. A word-processor operator is expected to know how to change diskettes and perform certain bail-out or recovery procedures. In the same way, any microcomputer operator should know at least something about the system he or she is running.

Like it or not, somebody in the office will have to become the computer "expert." There are certain routine operations, such as getting the system going in the morning, backing up data disks, and initializing disks, that simply require more knowledge of the system than running a good application program does. Once you're committed to using a computer system, your operation is going to get fouled up any time the computer is down. You can always depend on service personnel to solve your problems, but that's time-consuming and expensive. Things do go wrong, and sometimes they have *nothing* to do with situations described in the manuals.

Finally, somewhere along the line you will probably want to do something with your computer that is not part of a packaged software system. In that case, you have either to hire a programmer or write the program yourself. Once you have your data base established, it is possible to extract more information with relatively simple programs, and there is always the challenge and satisfaction of accomplishment in writing your own program.

No matter how a computer manufacturer advertises, realize that once you have a computer system online, either you or a designated person in your office is going to have to invest some time in learning about the computer in order to make best use of it.

• Hardware

This section deals with the types of hardware that are currently available, focusing on the microcomputer systems themselves (as opposed to peripherals). Please keep in mind that my aim is to suggest some factors to take into consideration when you're shopping for a microcomputer system, not to recommend one particular system or another.

The panoply of microcomputer systems and peripherals now on the market is staggering even to someone close to the field, and it would be impossible to mention one of everything within the scope of a book chapter. To give you an idea of what I mean, I thumbed through recent issues of eight personal-computer magazines and, without trying too hard, came up with the following list. Many of these manufacturers also offer a variety of models, and I must admit I had never heard the names of some until I saw their ads.

Cromemco	Osborne
North Star	Altos
Pertec	Vector Graphic
DEC	Ohio Scientific
Alpha Micro	Data General
NEC	Dynabyte
Billings	SD Systems
Smoke Signal	Xerox
Chieftain	Wang
IBM	Tarbell
Sharp	Heath
Hewlett-Packard	Victor
Superbrain	Canon
Durango	NNC
Digilog	TRS-80
Zenith	Texas Instruments
Apple	Atari
Commodore	MTI
Sinclair	TeleVideo
Savin	Integrated Business
Fortune	Computers
Archives	

The magazines from which I drew this list, incidentally, are *SoftSide, 80-U.S. Journal, Interface Age, Small Systems World, Compute!, Datamation, Personal Computing,* and *80 Micro.* The list of magazines, like the computer list, is not complete, but an indication of

the many that are available. These magazines, both in their advertisements and in their articles, are valuable sources of information about what's available on the market and what it costs.

These computers vary in cost as well as capabilities (there's some correlation), from the Timex Sinclair ZX81, selling for a hundred fifty dollars, to several of the higher-powered systems that start at around four thousand dollars and can go up to around ten thousand dollars when all the peripherals are added. The little Sinclair machine comes with 16K RAM, relies on you to supply a cassette recorder if you want to use one, requires the use of your television set as a display, and, while a fine means of learning about computers inexpensively, is not intended for business purposes. Others, such as Cromemco, IBM, DEC, and Data General, are intended for use as small business systems. The range in between is a continuous spectrum. Some of the machines are billed as general-purpose computers that can be used for virtually any purpose, and some have particular orientations. The Vector Graphic, for example, specializes in word processing but can be used in other ways. The Osborne is a general-purpose machine that folds into a carrying case and has built in everything necessary for communications via telephone. Given this range to select from, how do you figure out where to start?

Start Here

If you intend to use a microcomputer system for business applications, there are several features you should include. (I can't say *must* include, because you can do a lot with less. But doing with less means more work, more time, and inefficiency.)

1. As much RAM as the system will accommodate, probably a minimum of 32K.

2. Diskette or disk drive(s).

71

3. A printer.

You will want the maximum RAM that your system can accommodate because RAM is where all the action takes place. Having less than the maximum RAM will either limit what you can do or require more excursions to disk, and even the fastest disk is much, much slower than RAM. It is difficult to say what the maximum RAM for any system will be, due to variations among the systems. The eight-bit CPU chips used in the current crop of microcomputers have an inherent ability to address 64K memory locations; however, a portion of that 64K will be reserved for the system software (the operating system), and some machines feature memory management units (MMUs), which allow the system to handle more than 64K addresses.

You will want diskette or disk data storage because cassettes are too cumbersome for real data handling, and the "stringy floppies" or other fast-tape units limit the kinds of data handling you can do. There are many types of diskette or disk systems on the market, and the general trade-off among them is cost versus capacity. Speed figures in the equation too, but is within a limited range once you've made the cost/capacity decision. Hard-disk systems are faster than floppy diskettes and store more information on one unit.

You will want a printer because it would be impractical, for business applications, to transfer information from CRT screen to paper manually. There are so many kinds of printers that the one you need to meet your requirements will be a significant cost factor. Careful consideration of your needs could save you several hundred to a thousand dollars or more.

To start with, let's take a look at an absolute minimum. You can buy a keyboard/CPU unit capable of handling small business applications for as little as three hundred fifty dollars (which assumes your television set as a CRT monitor); you can buy diskette drives for about two hundred fifty dollars each (and you would want a minimum of two); you can buy a serviceable printer for about three hundred dollars. This means that you *could* set up a small business computer system for as little as eleven hundred fifty dollars. You can also buy a CPU unit for four thousand dollars, hard-disk drives for around four thousand dollars, and a fast line printer or professional letter-quality printer for around four thousand dollars. Top-end prices are much higher. I would recommend, however, that you use something more than the minimum possible, but I would suspect that you don't want to hand a computer dealer a blank check. A respectably middle-ground system capable of doing a reasonable amount of small-business computing would probably go for somewhere in the twenty-five-hundred-to-five-thousand-dollar range.

Now let's consider some of the other factors that might influence your decision:
1. Speeds.
2. Storage capacity.
3. Machine-inherent features.
4. Personal comfort.

Speeds

The speed at which a computer operates affects the amount of work it can do in any given time. While that statement may be obvious, the logic behind it is not: many computer operations seem to take place instantaneously. Remember that although a single operation is very fast, many computer functions involve repeating operations thousands of times. If one operation takes one hundred milliseconds (one-tenth second), then doing that operation ten thousand times will take one thousand seconds, or sixteen and two-thirds minutes.

A computer hobbyists' group recently ran a little "benchmark" test to compare system speeds. (A benchmark test pits differing machines against each other in performing the same task.) The test came from a problem that was published in the August 1981 issue of *Creative Computing:*

> A house number sign with a four-digit number printed on it fell down and broke in half. It was noted by the owner that if you added the two-digit number on one half of the sign to the two-digit number on the other half and then squared that total, you would have a number equal to the original four-digit number. Take the number 3025. 30 + 25 = 55. 55 squared = 3025.

The problem then goes on to ask how many other four-digit numbers would yield the same results if they were broken in half. A BASIC program that will check all the possibilities from 1000 to 9999 might be written as follows:

```
100 N = 1000
110 FOR X = 10 TO 99
120 FOR Y = 0 TO 99
130 IF (X + Y) × (X + Y) = N
    THEN PRINT N
140 N = N + 1
150 NEXT Y
160 NEXT X
170 END
```

Here's what the program statements mean:

100 Establish the starting sign number at 1000.
110 Count the two left-hand digits from 10 to 99.
120 For each value of the left digits, check all the possibilities of the two right digits from 0 (00) to 99.
130 Carry out the calculation and test the result. If the result meets the criterion, then print it.
140 Move to the next sign number.
150 Increment the Y count and go to try the next Y.
160 Increment the X count and go to try the next X.
170 End the program.

Now, a little arithmetic will tell you that if you're going to test all the numbers from 1000 through 9999 (that's *through,* not to) then you'll be testing nine thousand numbers. In the program, the outer loop—the X loop—counts from 10 through 99 (ninety values), and the inner loop—the Y loop—counts from 0 through 99 (one hundred values) for each X value. The number of times the calculation and test in the middle will be carried out is therefore 90 × 100 = 9000, as it should be.

And here are some representative results:

Machine	CPU Speed (MHz)	Time (min:sec)
Cromemco	4	1:08
North Star	4	1:13
TRS-80 Mod II	4	1:25
Apple	1.023	1:34
Pet	*	1:50
ZX81	*	2:22
TRS-80 Mod I	1.774	2:23

All these results were obtained using the BASIC interpreters built into the various machines, and BASIC interpreters in the microcomputers are inherently slow (in terms of computer speeds). By way of comparison, an IBM 3033 took 0.06 second to run the test, a microcomputer assembler version of the program took 0.32 second, and a compiled FORTRAN version of the program run on a TRS-80 Model I took 9.68 seconds.

I would also like to stress that these numbers are indicative, but far from absolute, for two reasons. First, you can sometimes use programming tricks—taking advantage of certain features inherent in a particular system—to speed up program execution. The same program in two slightly differing versions run on a TRS-80 Model I took 2 minutes 23 seconds in one case and 3 minutes 11 seconds in the other. Second, this particular test checks only *one* machine function. Operating systems

* Figures not available.

73

are often optimized in ways that speed up the more commonly used functions at the expense of the less commonly used ones. Testing some other function could change the order of the results shown above. (This particular test was also done just for fun and was far from scientifically controlled.)

But the point is this: even in the slowest result listed (2 minutes 23 seconds), each individual calculation took 143 seconds/9000 repetitions = 0.016 second (16 milliseconds), which would indeed be virtually instantaneous if one calculation were all you observed. But added together, the total time was quite noticeable.

(You can try running this program if you wish. While it is written in a general BASIC, it may need some adaptation for a particular system; also, it very likely could be rewritten to take advantage of some particular machine function. The answers, to be sure you got the program right, are 2025, 3025, and 9801.)

Storage Capacity

Storage capacity refers to the capacity of the diskette or disk system attached to the computer. While the storage components are peripherals, they are an integral part of the system, and you have to consider what your storage needs will be before you buy a system. What follow are my rules of thumb for estimating storage capacities. (Again, there are so many variables that only examination of a specific storage scheme will give definite answers.)

Three basic diskette or disk configurations are normally associated with microcomputer systems: 5¼-inch floppy diskettes, 8-inch floppy diskettes, and several kinds of small hard-disk systems. The configuration with the least capacity is a single-side, single-density, 35-track 5¼-inch diskette, which holds about 83 kilobytes. The hard-disk systems commonly come in 6-, 9.6-, and 20-megabyte configurations. Other configurations of the 5¼-inch and 8-inch floppies fall somewhere in between.

Chances are you will be using 5¼-inch floppies, the most common storage devices in use today with microcomputer systems. The operating systems for many of the microcomputers simply will not accommodate 8-inch floppies or hard disks. In discussing the 5¼-inch floppies, *single-side* means simply that only one side of the diskette is used to record data. *Single-density* is an arbitrary term that became necessary after somebody figured out how to double the capacity of the 5¼-inch floppies. Therefore, a double-sided diskette system will hold twice as much information as a single-sided one (though the two sides are treated by the operating system as two separate drives), and a double-density diskette will hold twice as much information as a single-density one.

The number of sides and the density are further complicated by having a varying number of tracks on the diskettes: thirty-five, forty, seventy, or eighty. Considering all these variations, I would not blame you for becoming confused in shopping for a diskette system (I know I did). The particular arrangement of sides, density, and tracks is not important unless you want your system to be compatible with someone else's. What's important is the total amount of storage space you need and the total amount of storage space that any particular scheme will provide. The next section in this chapter (application programs) contains an example of a ninety-six-byte record for a mailing-label program. You might want to look ahead to that discussion to give yourself a more concrete understanding of capacity.

Basically, one character equals one byte. My diskette system (single-side, single-density, forty-track) allows ninety-seven kilobytes of information on a formatted diskette (about five kilobytes are reserved for certain system information and a diskette directory). I could, therefore, store a maximum of about one thousand of the ninety-six-byte mailing-label records on one diskette. If I had an inventory file that used sixty-byte records, then I could store a maximum of about sixteen hundred inventory records on one diskette.

The practice becomes more complicated when you consider *all* the data you will be storing and the ways in which various programs will need to use it. Suppose, for example, that you want to run an accounting system that contains an inventory file, a customer-name-and-address file, an accounts-receivable file, and general-ledger files. When you run your invoices, you will need to draw on the inventory files for product numbers, descriptions, and prices; on the customer-name-and-address file; and on the general-ledger file to record the results of the accounts-receivable transaction. *Now* how many bytes of storage will you need online (available to the computer while a program is running)?

This situation is more complicated than the basic example, but far from hopeless. One maxim in programming (and one that works well in lots of other circumstances too) is that if a job seems impossibly large or complicated, then break it down into smaller tasks that you can handle. Let's take that approach here.

First, for the purposes of the accounting example, let's make a few assumptions to establish some of the facts that you will know from your actual business practice:

—you have 60 regular customers on file.
—you have 143 items in inventory.
—you maintain the last year's transactions on file for any customer.
—each customer has an average of 12 transactions during a year.

—you maintain 36 account codes in your general ledger.

Further, with a pencil and paper, you can determine how many bytes (characters) each record for the information listed above will require. Reasonable assumptions might be

—customer-name-and-address records are 96 bytes each.
—inventory records are 60 bytes each.
—each customer transaction requires 64 bytes.
—each general-ledger-account code requires 24 bytes.

Now all it takes is a little arithmetic:

60 customers $\times$ 96 bytes each = 5,760 bytes.

143 inventory items $\times$ 60 bytes each = 8,580 bytes.

60 customers $\times$ 12 transactions/year $\times$ 64 bytes/transaction = 46,080 bytes.

36 account codes $\times$ 24 bytes each = 864 bytes.

Summing up these individual requirements, we get a total of 61,284 bytes.

This makes it appear that you could use a single-side, single-density, 40-track diskette to store all your data. However, you must keep in mind when you are buying a computer system that you will probably have that system around for a while and that your needs are likely to change during the lifetime of the computer. If, for example, you expect to double your number of customers during the next couple of years and to increase the number of items you keep in stock, then the one-disk system we've described here won't suffice.

This example of calculating disk space requirements is only an example and takes into account only one kind of program that someone is likely to run in a business environment. You may be planning to use engineering or statistical programs that require much more data storage than accounting programs would. No matter how you go about it, plan your data storage and access needs on whatever program will require the most, and then allow some room for expansion. Virtually anyone who buys a microcomputer for one purpose soon finds many more uses for it.

I said earlier in this section on hardware that you would need a minimum of two diskette drives if you choose diskettes as your storage medium (and if the system you buy allows a variable number of diskette drives). A microcomputer system will operate with one diskette drive, but using only one drive limits storage capacity and makes operation more tedious than it would be with more than one. A portion of one diskette must be reserved for the *disk operating system* (DOS). The DOS contains both the system programming that makes the diskette drives work and utility programs for system management, and may either enhance the operating system stored in the computer's ROM or control system operation in lieu of a ROM.

A DOS occupies a fixed amount of disk space. Your programs, which will require a varying amount of space depending on just what they are, will also be stored on diskette. Therefore, with just one diskette drive, the amount of space available for data is the difference between the total space available on a diskette and what's required for storing DOS and programs. Using just one drive also necessitates swapping diskettes when backing up programs or data, or copying programs from one diskette to another, which means more operator intervention, more time, and more chances for mishaps.

The most common practice with the 5¼-inch floppies is to keep DOS and programs on one diskette and to leave other drives open for data diskettes. Application programs can be on other drives too. Thus, the more drives you have, the more programs and data you will be able to have online at any time. If you have few programs, a moderate amount of data, and several double-density diskettes, then you may be able to have your entire system online all the time. But it's more likely you will be changing diskettes for each application that you run.

If you use 8-inch floppies, then you'll be able to get much more information on any diskette, and if you go to one of the hard-disk systems, then you should be able to store everything—DOS, programs, and data—in one place. A hard-disk system would be the most efficient both because less time for operator intervention would be required and because the hard disks are physically faster than diskettes.

There is a matter of cost-per-byte economy. Four of the single-side, single-density, 40-track 5¼-inch diskette drives I mentioned as being relatively inexpensive (on the order of $250 each) would hold a total of about 400 kilobytes and would cost a total of $1,000. This configuration works out to about a quarter of a cent per byte. A small hard-disk system will hold a total of about 6 megabytes and cost around $2,000. The hard-disk configuration works out to about $\frac{3}{100}$ cent per byte. This calculation shows that the hard-disk system is considerably more economical on a cost-per-byte basis. The floppies are about 7½ times more expensive.

However, not all systems will accommodate four diskette drives, or 8-inch floppies, or hard-disk drives. Your final choice of storage medium will have to be based on what your microcomputer system will permit you to use, your overall storage needs, your notion of economy, and the amount of money you have available for your initial investment.

Machine-inherent Features

By machine-inherent features I mean such things as high-resolution graphics (lots of dots for plotting fine lines), color, and plug-in program modules. If these kinds of options cause one system to cost more than another, then, despite their gimmick value, take into account whether or not you will actually *need* them. If you are not going to do much scientific graphing on the CRT monitor, then there's probably no point in having high-resolution graphics. If you are going to be displaying nothing more than letters and numbers, then there's probably no reason to have color. Plug-in program modules have a certain attractiveness and ease of use, but they are entirely inflexible and may not suit your needs at all.

Buying a new computer is like buying a new car: The many available options may seem attractive, useful, or even a bargain under the blast of a salesman's heated pitch—but it may turn out that you will never use them. Just exactly what these machine-inherent features might be, how you regard them, and how you might use them to influence your decision will be entirely up to your needs, your tastes, and your pocketbook.

Personal Comfort

Finally, there's the matter of personal comfort. Remember that many of these machines are sold as *personal* computers, which implies that there's a good deal of personal feeling involved. If you're going to be spending measurable amounts of time with your computer, then you're going to want to be comfortable with it, just as you'd want to be comfortable with any other tool that you use frequently.

After you've done all the research and shopping necessary to find what you really and truly *need,* you may find three or four machines that will do the job for you, that cost about the same, but are just a little different. One may have a keyboard layout that appeals to you more. You may prefer a green screen to a gray one. You may simply like the shape and color of the case that one comes in more than another. One may have a language set that seems a little easier to use. You may find the angle of one display easier to look at than another. When it comes down to factors such as these, go with your gut feeling. It is, after all, *your* computer, and you are probably going to be spending a lot of time with it. Pick the one that suits you.

• Applications

If you intend to use your computer primarily for business, or if you at least intend to have it double as a business tool, then you will probably want some kind of business-oriented programs to make the machine perform the tasks you have in mind. You can, of course, always write your own specialized programs to get just exactly the results you want, but if you are new to computers, it's likely that writing complex programs where mistakes could be costly will be beyond you for a while.

There are available on the market packaged, ready-to-go programs for a variety of applications ranging from the most commonly used, such as word processing and general-ledger bookkeeping, to many that are much more specialized, such as statistical calculations, legal reference systems, and computational packages for virtually all the engineering professions. Actually, there are so many off-the-shelf programs available that it would be difficult simply to name them all here, let alone describe any in detail. Here's a small sample to give you some idea:

Word processing	Data-base managers
—spellers	Accounting systems
Mailing list	—restaurant-payroll
Stock-market analysis	—legal
Tax packages	—medical
Real-estate analysis	Intelligent terminal
Scheduling	Calculating programs
(CPM/PERT)	System utilities

Financial modeling   Agricultural
Decision makers   management
Statistics   Engineering

If you are curious about how much is on the software market, you can find thick volumes in some libraries and computer stores that contain nothing but the names of programs and abstracts of their functions. I think it would, however, be helpful to describe just a few of the more common types of programs in terms of both what they do and how they work.

Data-base Managers

A data-base manager, well, manages your data base. Let's backtrack just a little and talk about data and data bases.

You already know that computers operate on data. Data is nothing more than the raw information that you put in: part numbers, prices, wages, hours, structural stress measurements, names and addresses, fluid flow in a manufacturing process, the contents of your freezer—you name it. It's all data.

A data base, despite its higher-flung definitions, is simply the collection of all the data you need to perform a specific chore. For a mailing-list program, the data base would be a collection of names and addresses; for a payroll program, employee names, social-security numbers, hourly rates, hours worked, tax rates, deductions, and so forth.

To describe the elements of data processing in a bit more detail, let's first establish a hierarchy of terms, then explain each term and fit it into a whole. Here are the terms:

character
field
record
file
data base

A *character* is just that: one individual letter or number (one byte) of information.

A *field* is the collection of characters that represents one basic unit of information. To use a mailing-list example again, the collection of characters that represents a person's name would be the name field; the characters that make up the address would be the address field, and so on. What makes up a field is determined by the uses to which the data is to be put and how it will be accessed by the program that uses it. In a mailing-list program, the name field might be subdivided into first-name field and last-name field for searching or sorting (alphabetizing), and a zip-code field might be separated out for the same reasons. Since it is unlikely that the street number itself (the 123 in 123 Main Street) would ever be needed, it would be illogical and a waste of memory and program execution time to create a separate field for it.

A *record* is made up of all the fields associated with the key item of interest. A mailing-list record might therefore consist of name field and address field. In an inventory program, the specific item of interest would be a particular part, and the record associated with it might consist of fields for part number, part name, purchase price, sale price, desired quantity in stock, actual quantity in stock, number sold same month last year, and number sold to date this month.

A *file* is the collection of all the records associated with one activity: all the name and address records (which might be called the mailing-list file) or all the part-number records (the inventory file).

Finally, then, the *data base* is a collection of all the files needed for any larger function. In the case of a manufacturing firm, the data base associated with accounting might consist of an inventory file, a payroll file, an accounts-receivable file, and an accounts-payable file, all linked together by a general-ledger file.

All this can be thought of in terms of a

more familiar system using pieces of paper, folders, and filing cabinets. The data base would be all the file cabinets holding the information for a function; the files would be the individual drawers in the file cabinets; the records would be the folders in the drawers, the fields would be the pieces of paper in the folders, and the characters would be the typed or handwritten characters on the pieces of paper.

You should also by now be able to see that data bases can contain huge amounts of information—information that has to be originated, stroke by stroke, by a person sitting at a keyboard. Also, some of the information in a data base is going to change with time. Data is necessary, and data entry and maintenance are time-consuming and costly. It therefore stands to reason that once you have a data base established, you don't want it to get messed up, and that anything that can make data entry and maintenance easier will save time and money. This is where data-base managers come in.

To help make this abstract discussion a little more concrete, let's look at an example: I use my computer to maintain a membership list for a club to which I belong. The membership program produces mailing labels (in zip-code order) for the club newsletter each month and generates a membership status record—total number of members, current for any month, lapsed for any month, and so forth, in alphabetical order. I set up a 96-byte record for the information necessary to carry out the required functions (the top line is the record; below it are position numbers of the fields in the record):

The information in the 96-byte record can also be tabulated like this:

FIELD NAME	LENGTH	POSITION IN RECORD
Membership type	1	1
Expiration date	4	2 – 5
Name	20	6 – 25
Street address	30	26 – 55
City	20	56 – 75
State	2	76 – 77
Zip code	9	78 – 86
Date joined	6	87 – 92
Alpha sort code	4	93 – 96

I created these particular fields for specific reasons: the membership code is used to determine how many issues of the newsletter a person gets; the expiration date is used to flag the status list for members who are about to lapse; the name and the address are used on the mailing labels; the date joined is kept as a record of a member's longevity in the club; an alphabetical sort code is used instead of breaking up the name field into first-name and last-name fields.

If you are completely new to computers, all this might look like an unwarranted amount of detail. It is not, and whenever you set up a data base, you will have to go through the same kind of exercise. Data structure—the way records and files are organized—is important. You do not want to waste any space in data storage, and you want the data organized in an optimal way for use by the computer. Poorly organized data can cost processing time. Each record must be the same length (hence the blank spaces in the name and address fields) to allow addition, deletion,

```
M1084John J. Jones     123 Main St., Apt. 11        Smithtown       CA912340000021781J058
00000000011111111112222222222333333333344444444445555555555666666666677777777778888888889999999
12345678901234567890123456789012345678901234567890123456789012345678901234567890123456
```

searching, and sorting, and the various fields must occupy the same relative positions in each record so that they can be isolated by the computer.

The biggest advantage of data-base managers is that they take care of a lot of the picky work for you, and you don't have to know anything about programming to use them. They are, in a sense, programs that write programs for you. About all you have to know is what information you want a record to contain, how you want the fields defined, and how long you want each field to be. In establishing the data base, the data-base manager should ask questions in plain English: How many fields? What is the name of the first field? How long is it? Is it alphabetic or numeric? Which one is the key field? And so on. The data-base manager will then assemble the fields into records and the records into files without any further worry on your part.

Data-base managers come in numerous forms and offer many options. Any data-base manager must at *least* allow you to define your fields (records and files); permit you to add, delete, and change records; sort the file according to a key field (last name, part number, or zip code); and search the file on any field. The second advantage to using a data-base manager is that it will allow you to use just one program to maintain any file, even though you may have any number of separate programs that use the files in various ways.

The higher-powered (and more costly and more memory-consuming) data-base managers allow a broad range of capabilities. You may be able to use them to manipulate your files in many ways. For example, from a lengthy mailing-list file, you could print just those names in a specified zip code or range of zip codes. You might be able to sort the file by zip code with names alphabetized within zip codes. You could cull sales records to pick out the ten best sellers during a specified period of time and sum up the total sales. Best of all, you might be able to extract pieces of information from two or more files to create a new file entirely. The most powerful of the data-base managers will permit you to give, in plain English, specifications for virtually any kind of report you might need.

If you don't think you're going to want to write your own, limited data-entry and file-maintenance routines into your programs, or if someone who is unfamiliar with programming will be operating your system, then you might want to get a data-base manager. If you are going to do a lot of file manipulation, the data-base manager could be your most fundamental and versatile tool. Before you buy one, be as sure as you can of all the uses you might want to put it to, and choose well. A good data-base manager could save you much time and work and should be useful for as long as you have your computer system.

• Word Processors

Word processing, along with "download," is one of the uglier terms to emerge from computerdom, but it is a phrase that is much heard these days. There are many new "word processors" on the market challenging the older brands, and virtually every microcomputer vendor offers a word-processing package with his product. More than likely, everyone who has crossed paths with the concept understands that a word processor is, at the very least, a fancy electronic typewriter. True, but a word processor is much more than that, and is usually a source of amazement and delight to even the most seasoned writer who has accumulated a lifetime of notches in his ancient Royal or Smith-Corona.

The first step in understanding word processing is to abandon the notion that a word processor is some kind of special machine. It is not: it is a microcomputer that is programmed to carry out a special function. Recall that a computer is a machine that can manipulate symbols electronically. In the case of word processing, the symbols are letters typed in from a keyboard. It's as simple as that. The letters and words, like any other data, are then "processed" by the computer. In other words, once the data is in the computer, you can shuffle it around however you like without ever having to retype anything. You might want to consider a word processor as a kind of correction tape, scissors, and paste pot all rolled up in one package.

For this discussion, let's divide the world of word processors into two large groups: cursor-oriented systems and line-oriented systems, terms I'll explain shortly. There are variations on the theme (a page-oriented system, for example, provides a combination of cursor-oriented and line-oriented functions), but these two distinctions will give you a measure by which to judge a word-processing system. Any word processor, regardless of how it is billed, has two basic elements to its programming: an editor and a formatter.

The editor is the data-entry portion of the program. It is the means by which you get the words and formatting commands into the computer and the means by which you can make corrections, changes, additions, deletions, or gross manipulations of the text. The text you are entering or working with is displayed on a CRT screen so that you can see it. As long as you're using the editor, it's like an electronic blackboard: you can erase or change or whatever you want, and nothing is committed to paper until you call up the formatter. The formatter is the output portion of the program. It combs through the data input via the editor and counts characters for line spacing; reacts to the formatting commands to change margins, underline portions of the text, and skip to new pages; and outputs the text to a printer. When the formatter is working, there may or may not be an equivalent screen display.

What does a word processor actually do?

Here is a list of functions that any word processor should perform. Every word-processor vendor has some special function that he will tout loudly, but any word processor worth its salt should do at least these things:

From the editor,

—Overstriking. As you are entering text, you should be able, at least in the line you're working on, to backspace and replace an incorrect character with a correct one.

—Deleting. You should be able with the stroke of a key, to delete a character, a word, perhaps a paragraph, and certainly a specified block of text of any length.

—Inserting. The editor should allow you to insert a single character, new words and sentences, or whole specified blocks of text. The feature to insert blocks of text should also allow you to repeatedly insert (duplicate) the text.

—Moving. You should be able to move (exchange) blocks of text.

—Searching. You should be able to search the text for any specified string: a word or group of words. This is handy in making corrections, because you can ask the computer to search for the erroneous entry.

—Global replace or delete. The word global means that a string is found and replaced or deleted in all the text at hand. If, for example, the name of the device that for years has been known as a "widget" suddenly is henceforth to be called a "frammis," you should be able to instruct the computer to find all occurrences of "widget" and replace each one with "frammis." Similarly, you could delete all references to widgets.

With formatting commands,

—Set margins. Just like a typewriter, except that the margins are moved in and out for such things as inset quotes or lists as the output is printed.

—Justify. You should be able to justify text (have smooth margins both right and left) if you wish.

—Center text. Have the computer automatically center headings or anything else you wish.

—Supply headers and footers. The formatter should allow you automatically to have a header, footer, or both placed on each page.

—Number pages. The system should number pages automatically. Page numbers can usually be incorporated into headers or footers.

And so forth. Again, this is a description of the minimal functions of a word processor. Most of them will do more. You may be able, for example, to justify columns of numbers automatically, have the formatter repeat text with pauses for insertion (such as typing "personalized" form letters), or, with special commands, create a "window" for illustrations to be inserted. Some of the fancier word processors also have a built-in "calculator" function that will sum up the column of numbers that it automatically justifies. (Personally, I find it ironic that a word processor should tout a calculator function—after all, the word processor is basically a specialized use of a piece of equipment that's normally thought of as a calculating machine.)

The terms *cursor-oriented* and *line-oriented* refer to the way you locate your position in the text in order to give the system commands. With a cursor-oriented system, what you see on the screen is just lines of text. You can position the cursor—usually a blinking blob of light on the screen—wherever you want, with keys usually indicated by up, down, right, and left arrows. As the cursor moves beyond the limits of the text on display at the moment, new text will be moved (scrolled) onto the screen. When you've positioned the cursor exactly where you want it, then you can overstrike or issue commands to insert or delete. With a line-oriented system, each line of text on the screen has a number. To make changes, you cannot simply position the cursor, but must instead call up the line you want by number; to move blocks of text, you must specify them by number.

It may seem that a cursor-oriented system would be the best way to go because of its ease of use. Perhaps, but, as always, there are trade-offs. Generally, the capacity of a cursor-oriented system is limited to the amount of text that can be retained in RAM, which, with many microcomputer systems, may be on the order of 32K characters, or about ten single-spaced pages. This means that the amount of text you may be able to handle at one time would best be suited to long letters or short reports. Naturally, many ten-page chunks of text may be strung together, but it will usually be up to you to do the file manipulation necessary to arrange the chunks in a convenient way (to introduce page breaks or stop a file at the end of a page).

Line-oriented systems are constructed as they are because the line numbers refer to records on file on a disk, so the amount of text you can consider as one chunk may be virtually unlimited, depending on your disk capacity. Any tediousness in line editing may be more than compensated for by the ability to consider a huge amount of text in one unit, make very large text moves, merge or chain very large files, and have the whole works print out on one command. If your word-processing needs require you routinely to produce large reports or even books, then a line-oriented system may suit you better.

By now you know that the capacity and versatility of a word-processing system is a function of cost. You can buy or assemble the components of a system capable of handling perhaps 32K of text and producing draft copy (that is, using a dot-matrix printer) for as little as two thousand dollars. But as we mentioned in the section on peripherals, a top-of-the-line letter-quality printer can cost about forty-five hundred dollars alone. If you want to handle large amounts of text and get camera-ready printout with boldface, underscoring, proportional spacing, superscripts, and subscripts, you'll have to pay more for it.

In summary, the caveat for word processors is the same as for everything else: Know what your requirements are, shop, and don't be oversold—or undersold—by some fast-talking computer salesman.

Intelligent Terminals

The first question you may have is, "What, in this context, are terminals?" Somewhere you have probably seen somebody working at a keyboard and CRT display where there seemed to be no computer. This may have been in a business such as an insurance company, where several people in an office were entering data from keyboards at their desks; or where a computer was even less evident, such as when buying tickets at an airline counter. In both of these situations, the keyboards and CRT displays at which the people were working, situated at some distance from the computers to which they were connected, are referred to as terminals. In particular, these are called dumb terminals, because they can do nothing but send data to the host computer or echo back what the host sends to them. They are, in fact, under the control of the host computer.

An intelligent terminal, on the other hand, while it talks to the host computer just like a dumb terminal, is under its own program control and can do more than echo what the host tells it to. An intelligent terminal program is one that makes a stand-alone microcomputer system act like an intelligent terminal.

The second question you may have is, "But if I have my own computer, then why would I want to make it act like only a terminal?" There can be several reasons.

The main reason is to allow you to connect your computer by telephone lines to some other computer: a time-shared system in your community, one of the large communications networks such as The Source or CompuServe, or the microcomputer of a friend (though his will probably have to be the same type as yours). There are also a number of hobby nets where individuals use their home computers as bulletin boards for local users' groups. You might want to hook up to a local time-share system to take advantage of its greater file-storage capacity or some other feature it has that your system doesn't, or to use the time-share system as a middle ground through which you can pass data to someone else who can also connect to it. The communications networks offer a variety of services such as up-to-the-minute stock-market information, user-accessible programs such as statistical analyses, and electronic mail. If you can hook up with a friend on the other side of town (or the other side of the continent, if you're willing to pay the long-distance charges), you can pass programs or data back and forth directly, or perhaps play a game for two. The hobby nets are something like small versions of the communications networks, and allow you to read messages on the system such as the location of the next users' group meeting or items for sale, or to post your own message for all to read or for a particular individual.

I mentioned the necessity of a telephone connection almost in passing, but it is not something that can be overlooked. In order to be able to use an intelligent-terminal program, you will need two pieces of hardware: In the computer, you must have a device that will convert information into a serial format (RS-232C is the most common one). Outside the computer, you must have a modem. Let's consider these two items one at a time.

You learned in Chapter 2 that most microcomputers store and work with information represented by eight-bit binary bytes, and that alphanumeric characters—letters, numbers, punctuation marks, and special characters—

may be represented with standard encoding schemes (EBCDIC and ASCII). Most microcomputers use ASCII for alphanumeric coding. The ASCII code for the letter *A* can be looked at this way:

Character: A

ASCII code: 41

Binary: 00101001

The microcomputers also work with parallel circuitry, which means if you were a chip in the computer you would see the letter *A* coming at you just as it's shown above, with all eight 0's and 1's lined up side by side. Perhaps the easiest way to visualize the need for a parallel-to-serial converter (the RS-232 device) is to consider how hard it would be to shove eight bits side by side through a single telephone wire. They must instead be pumped out one by one, first a 0, then another 0, then a 1, and so on, and that's what the RS-232 circuitry does. It takes the eight-bit parallel byte and puts it out one bit at a time through a separate port.

But a telephone can't understand 0's and 1's, and that's why the modem is necessary. The modem (stands for MOdulator-DEModulator) turns each 0 into one tone and each 1 into another tone (modulates the signal). The tones are then transmitted over the telephone lines, and a modem on the receiving end turns them back into 0's and 1's (demodulates the signal) for the receiving computer (the process is actually a bit more complicated, but this, in general, is how it works).

Having cleared some of the background and hardware out of the way, let's get back to intelligent-terminal programs. The heart of any terminal program—intelligent or dumb—is software that takes your keyboard strokes and routes them out through the telephone and, conversely, takes information coming in over the telephone and converts it to readable characters on your CRT screen. What else

might you expect an intelligent-terminal program to do?

—Log you onto a system automatically. On the time-share systems, you pay for the computer time you use, and even on the hobby nets there has to be some way to tell one caller from another. This is done with a log-on message, which normally includes an account number that separates your computer time out for billing. A source log-on message takes the form

ID ACCOUNT ⌀ PASSWORD

A local time-share system I worked on recently required a log-on that looked like

HELLO GROUP.X/GO;TERM=N

Some of the hobby nets I check into occasionally ask for name and address in a specific format.

If you sign onto a remote system frequently, you will soon tire of typing the same old log-on message, and it often seems you are more prone to making mistakes the more you do it. An intelligent-terminal program might therefore allow you to store a log-on message. When you press the right key, the program transmits the message and gets you logged onto the system automatically.

—Permit you to *download* or *upload* files. If all you can do is watch incoming information go by on your screen, then your remote computer communications will be fleeting and impermanent (and perhaps pointless). It stands to reason that if you are receiving important information, then you will want to store it. Conversely, plinking in your information one keystroke at a time (especially if you're not a very fast typist) can be both tedious and costly, since you will be paying both computer connect time and normal telephone charges. An intelligent-terminal program may therefore offer you the capability to hold and store incoming information (download) or to transmit automatically (upload) information you've previously stored when you're *not* hooked up to the telephone. For downloading, the program will hold a certain amount of information in a RAM buffer, then write it out to a diskette file upon command. For uploading, the program will allow you to load a diskette file into the RAM buffer and then transmit it at the maximum speed the system will allow. Most often, information that is uploaded or downloaded is created or used by a program other than the terminal program (and may even *be* a program). The intelligent-terminal program is a transmission medium, a means rather than an end.

—Allow your microcomputer to function as the host computer. This feature is important if you think you may want to link your computer with a friend's. It will allow the communication to take place if all he has is a dumb-terminal program, and besides, it's fun to play host once in a while.

—Permit you to route incoming information to a printer.

—Allow you to transmit special characters not found on your keyboard. This is important, especially if your keyboard doesn't have a CONTROL (CTL or CNTL) key. Control-Q, for example, is a universal "pause" signal from terminal to host, and Control-S is the universal "restart" signal. There may also be others peculiar to the host system you're working with.

As with all software, various intelligent-terminal programs may well sport differing features, and what I've listed here is intended to be descriptive rather than prescriptive. Just be sure that you get a program that will do everything you want it to.

Similarly, if you are going to go in for telecommunications, be sure to get a modem that will do what you want it to. Modems have two controls on them, one relating to their transmit/receive function, and one relating to a line/local function. The trans-

mit/receive switch will be labeled "originate" and "answer." If you get an "originate only" modem, you will always have to play the role of terminal in any exchange. A friend could not call you and ask you to play host to his terminal. The line/local control will be labeled "full duplex" and "half duplex." In order to carry out communications with a host, you must have full-duplex capability. (What you see on your screen in these communications is not an output direct from your keyboard, but an echo of what the host is receiving. If you have a bad connection, it is possible that you will press one key on your keyboard but see another character on the screen.) Modems fall into two broad categories: automatic and acoustic, sometimes called acoustic couplers. With an automatic modem, all connections are made directly and you do not need a telephone. With an acoustic coupler, you physically place a telephone handset into a padded receptacle. The prices of modems within each category vary so slightly that a bargain-basement modem just isn't worth it.

While some of the higher-priced computers offer RS-232 transmission rates of 1,200 baud, the most common speed is 300 baud. Baud means bits per second, and you know that each character requires eight bits. The information exchange rate, in terms of characters per second, is therefore 300 ÷ 8, or 37.5. This corresponds to a typing rate of 450 words per minute. If you are considering transferring large amounts of data via phone lines at 300 baud, consider also how long it would take you to read the same data at 450 words per minute. In other words, lightning-like computer speeds just don't apply to telephone lines (and it is the telephone lines that are the limiting factor). I recently wrote a manual that was 269 kilobytes in length—about 130 single-spaced pages of computer print—using a client's account on a time-share system. Arithmetic says that ideal transmission of that amount of data at 300 baud would require two hours; as a matter of fact, what with calling up files and waiting for pauses in the time-share computer and so forth, it took four hours to download the text to my system.

Accounting Programs

Computers are reputed to do two things extremely well: store and manipulate information, and perform arithmetic. Businesses of all types require a certain amount of bookkeeping, which by its nature depends upon the storage and retrieval of financial data and the performance of arithmetic. It is therefore perfectly logical that if the computer was invented on Day 1, then by noon of Day 2 a programmer rushed the first accounting programs to market.

It's easy to see that a very large company would benefit from having its accounting chores performed by a computer. But remember that we're talking about microsystems, computer systems which, while available at reasonable cost (and let's assume that a starter system that would handle the accounting for a small business will sell in the range of twenty-five hundred to five thousand dollars), also have an upper limit on their practicality. If you're reading this book to gain an introduction to computers, then you are probably also deciding whether or not to buy one. If you are responsible for a company with a large inventory and several hundred employees, then it would be impractical for you to consider using a microcomputer for the company's accounting. Similarly, if you run a company with a limited inventory and only four employees, then it probably would not pay you to invest in a computer solely to do your bookkeeping. It's in the middle ground, about twenty employees, that the prospect of having a machine to take care of the arithmetic and paperwork becomes attractive.

In California's Silicon Valley, new companies are a way of life. One person gets an idea, or a couple of college buddies get together to try a scheme, and a new company is born. At first, the boss takes care of everything, and if employees are hired, they usually are directly involved in creating, manufacturing, or selling the product, so their salaries are normally compensated for in increased sales. At some point, however, the boss inevitably finds that he has become too busy with the details of company management to function effectively, so he hires an assistant. That first assistant inevitably becomes the complete administrative arm of the company, taking care of everything from being receptionist and secretary to making coffee, buying and lugging office supplies around, handling time cards, dealing with vendors, washing windows, and doing the bookkeeping. If the company proves successful, inventory increases, the payroll grows, and the assistant becomes swamped.

Here the boss reaches his crux: Another person hired solely to take care of bookkeeping is pure overhead; his whole pricing structure is suddenly altered, and he may lose his competitive edge. A microcomputer system that will handle the accounting may cost five thousand dollars. It will be a one-time expense, can be depreciated on taxes, and may be used for other functions. Another employee, even part-time, will cost at least as much as the computer, and will be an ongoing expense. *But* if the assistant can learn to run the computer and still have time for other chores, then the boss won't have to add another salary to the payroll and everyone comes out ahead.

The accounting systems for microcomputers (and, actually, for larger computers too) generally come in modules, partly so that they can be installed a piece at a time and partly so that a user can add them to his system in a financially attractive way. The programs within accounting modules may be arranged in various ways, but a complete system should contain

—a general ledger,
—accounts payable,
—accounts receivable,
—payroll, and
—inventory.

While I've listed these accounting functions in what may seem to be a more or less logical hierarchy, they usually are not incorporated into a computer system in that same order. (Don't worry if yours is a service-oriented business that does not maintain an inventory. We'll get to that in a moment.) The main reason that the modules don't come online starting with the general ledger is that a financial data base has to be established before the accounting system can be brought into full play. If you started with the general ledger, you would in theory have your electronic bookkeeper all set to go—except that a human being would have to enter every transaction from a keyboard, which wouldn't be much of a step away from cuff protectors and quill pens.

Under most circumstances, the inventory or a combination of inventory and accounts receivable would be added first. Not only is it nice to have the computer take over the drudgery of preparing invoices, but the data base can be built through use, rather than having to take a separate step to key in nothing but data. The process of adding an inventory/accounts-receivable package might go something like this: The first time the program is used, the operator would key in the customers' names and addresses, the items and quantities purchased, and associated part numbers and sales prices. About all the computer would do is carry out the extensions, sum up the totals, and print the invoices. But two other, less visible things happen at the same time: the customers' names and addresses go into a customer file, along with a

sales history if that was part of the package, and the part numbers, item descriptions, quantities sold, and sales prices go into inventory files. Then, the next time (and all succeeding times) the program is run, the operator would have to key in only the customer name or number to get full address and other particulars, and only the part number to get its description and sales price. Obviously, the customers' sales histories and inventory could be updated with each run.

The next module to be added could be accounts payable, which would complete the other half of the inventory process. The first time the accounts payable was run, the operator would key in vendors' names and addresses and purchase prices, and all the computer would do is carry out the arithmetic and print the checks. The vendors' names and addresses would go off to the vendors' file, and the purchase prices of items would be added to the inventory files. Succeeding runs of the accounts-payable program would work analogously to the accounts-receivable program. And with the inventory data now substantially complete, separate inventory functions could be invoked to add in the actual quantity of items on hand, the desired number on hand, and any other applicable information.

With inventory, accounts receivable, and accounts payable in place, the general ledger can be added. It should stand to reason that one prime function of the general ledger is to draw on the payable and receivable files and carry out the general-ledger accounting associated with them with no further keyboard input from an operator. Other items associated with the general-ledger bookkeeping would, however, be keyed in.

If the most commonly thought-of trio of accounting programs is accounts receivable (with inventory), accounts payable, and general ledger, then payroll comes in as a certain fourth. Many small businessmen feel that getting a payroll system online first would be easiest and save them the greatest amount of time. Not necessarily. While accounts receivable, accounts payable, and a general ledger all work together nicely and logically, payroll really functions as a separate step in the accounting process. Certainly payroll expenses will be transferred to a general ledger, but they are not, particularly where overhead personnel are concerned, as intimately linked with an inventory and production operation as the steps involving A/R, A/P, and GL: A payroll program brought online by itself does nothing to establish a data base. And a payroll program by itself tends to create a security problem, because all the company's detailed wage and salary information just sits there, available, but out of context. It is for these reasons that payroll, while a temptation to be first, is listed last in the accounting hierarchy.

A good payroll program should do much more than just print out paychecks and leave a stub record behind. Payrolls tend to get complicated quickly, with differing wages for various jobs, overtime, vacation, sick pay, and insurance and tax deductions, to say the least. The payroll program you select should have the capability to handle all the payroll variations you actually experience and should also take care of such chores as quarterly reporting for taxes, W-2 forms, and payment histories.

Recall how this section on accounting programs was prefaced: Computers store and manipulate information as well as perform arithmetic. In addition to doing the arithmetic, an accounting package builds a company's financial data base, and that data base contains information that can be used for purposes other than accounting: management, planning, and forecasting, for example. This information is, of course, available in a manual bookkeeping system, but retrieving it is tedious, and preparing any kind of report based on it requires a separate step and a good deal of personnel time. The second attractive feature of accounting programs is, therefore, their report-generating capabilities. You should, with just a few keystrokes, be able to get information back out of the system rapidly and conveniently. The reporting capabilities built into accounting systems vary with the systems, but here are some examples of the kinds of things you might find:

In accounts receivable: an aged receivables report, sales histories by customer or salesman, cash-flow forecasts.

In inventory: sales histories of stock items, quantities of stock on hand, cost analyses.

In accounts payable: an aged payables report, vendor histories, cash-flow forecast.

In general ledger: income statement, deposit register, check register, balance sheet.

In payroll: quarterly reporting for taxes, payment histories.

Throughout: audit trails so that you can trace the progress of a transaction.

For service-oriented companies that don't maintain an inventory or have the same flow of payables as a manufacturing or wholesale firm, there are accounting systems that allow for invoicing based on services rendered. In their most general forms, accounting programs such as these can be applied to law offices, public-relations firms, advertising agencies, and similar businesses. There are also specialized service-oriented accounting programs that are geared to deal with the specific requirements of professional offices such as law, medicine, and dentistry.

Whatever your specific accounting needs may be, there are two other factors that should be included in your consideration of accounting systems: customization and support.

Most of the general accounting needs of businesses are the same regardless of the product involved, but in order for any accounting program to perform according to your specific needs, you will want to be able to customize it to some degree. The program you select should, for example, allow you to include your company name on any of the reports, be flexible enough to be able to handle any odd-ball parts descriptions you may have, be compatible with your system of parts numbering, and so forth. Your accounting system should also provide you with enough information about it so that you can understand and get at the data base with specialized programs of your own that are clearly outside the claims or responsibilities of the vendor. One hallmark of a good accounting program (indeed, of *any* good application program) is its ability to adapt to your needs, rather than force you to deal with the idiosyncrasies of a shortsighted programmer. Customization should be as much a part of an accounting program as its ability to do arithmetic, so be sure that it's there and that it is flexible enough for your needs.

Support, in software terms, is the service provided by the vendor in keeping his programs compatible with your needs. Certainly it is a cost factor in the price of an accounting system, and may not necessarily be included.

At the low end of the scale, you can buy a software system and then be entirely on your own for figuring out how to use it. At the high end, the vendor will work with you in customizing the general package to your needs and then will continue support by making further changes in his software to keep pace with changing situations in your company. Ongoing support is often sold as a separate option, just as service contracts are available for computer systems and home appliances.

It should go without saying that computerized accounting systems should not be taken lightly. If you are going to entrust your company's financial record keeping to a computer system, then you will want to be very sure that the system will do exactly what you want it to do and that you have complete control over it. Getting information scrambled or having the whole system fail at a crucial time is no joke. An initially inexpensive accounting system could, in the long run, turn out to be costly indeed. Shop wisely for accounting packages, and be sure you are thoroughly satisfied *before* you commit yourself.

10

FUN AND GAMES

Almost from the time the first practical computer began operating, people played games with it. Programmers, easily bored with such prosaic matters as actuarial tables, meteorological data, and atomic-energy formulas, amused themselves by playing chess, checkers, and tic-tac-toe with computers. Kent Porter, in his excellent and highly recommended book *Computers Made Really Simple* (New York: Thomas Y. Crowell Company, 1976), wrote:

> In 1952, a man was heard on the radio describing the capabilities of the machine he supervised, and one of his comments was that it was unbeatable at tic-tac-toe. My own father had a comment that seems to summarize the overall feeling of America at that point in the computer's infancy: "It seems pretty silly to me to spend millions of dollars to build a machine to play tic-tac-toe."

Obviously—and understandably—the senior Mr. Porter had no way of foretelling, any more than the rest of us did, that this machine that played tic-tac-toe would change the shape of the world.

Nevertheless, the underlying philosophy of that comment is as true today for the would-be purchaser of a microcomputer as it was in the 1950s. Even the most rudimentary microcomputer is expensive in comparison to a chess set, a deck of cards, electronic video games, and a lot of other objects that can be used for amusement. Does the price justify the game-playing end? The answer is that it does if you think it does. This is, after all, a moral argument and one that can be applied to a trip to Las Vegas, an expensive hi-fi system, a limousine, an original work of art, or anything else for which there exists a cheaper, functional substitute that will readily fulfill the need. Obviously, then, need is not the issue. If your interests in a microcomputer rest solely in the areas of amusement, then whether to indulge yourself becomes a question to be debated between you, your finances, and whoever else in the world you may feel obliged to answer to. Just leave me out of it.

But the computer as game player suggests a much more subtle, perhaps even a philosophical, question. One writer has described the computer as an idiot. It cannot think. It cannot act on its own. It has no emotions, no feelings, no sense of right or wrong. No matter what the science fiction writers and filmmakers say, a computer has no will of its own; it is only a tool of humankind. If that is true, isn't asking a computer to play a game something like asking a camera to take a good picture? A camera will photograph whatever it is told to photograph. If it is a fancy camera, it will adjust itself to the lighting conditions and make a proper exposure. But it will photograph the ugly and the beautiful with complete equanimity. It will take a well-composed picture as well as a badly composed one. It will photograph the most inspiring religious image or the filthiest pornography. The aesthetic quality of a photograph depends not on the camera, but on the photographer. Similarly, how can a computer play a better game of chess or tic-tac-toe than a person can? We have already seen the answer: the machine operates logically, it makes comparisons among pieces of data, then makes decisions on the basis of those comparisons, and does it all at speeds that are inconceivable to most human minds. But isn't that the same as thinking? When a person makes a decision, doesn't that involve a process of taking various bits of data, weighing and comparing them, and making the necessary decision accordingly? Well, yes and no. At least one of the differences between a computer and a person is that the computer can never have certain types of data that the human mind contains. If a computer lets you win, it is not because the computer likes you or feels pity for you, but because it has been programmed to let you win. If a computer beats you every time, it is not because the machine hates you, but because it has more data, logic, and speed than you have. I once played tic-tac-toe with a microcomputer. At the outset, the machine offered me a range of difficulty, on a scale of 0 to 9, from which to choose. When I chose the low end of the difficulty scale, I won just about every game. When I chose the high end of the difficulty scale, I lost every time. No emotion was involved, at least not on the computer's part. Even when the CRT on which the games were displayed printed out, YOU LOSE AGAIN, DUMMY, the machine was only doing what it was programmed to do, a realization that kept me from putting my fist through its immobile face.

Computer games, then, offer at least three benefits: (1) they amuse; (2) they can be educational; and (3) they can demonstrate very effectively to the average layman, who has neither interest in nor knowledge of computers, just how frail and faulty a thing the human brain is.

• Electronic Diversions

In a sense, the very act of acquiring a microcomputer and expanding upon it is a kind of game. After all, home computing began as a hobby and still gets much of its impetus from hobbyists.

An almost perfect marriage has taken place between amateur radio hobbyists and personal computer hobbyists. In terms of cost, availability of supplies and materials, and compatibility with home workshops, the two areas are very much alike. Inevitably, a number of hobbyists have combined the two fields. Some have used their microcomputers to convert messages to and from Morse code, enabling the transmission of as many as a thousand words per minute. In other operations, the microcomputer takes the place of the human station operator. Using the radio, the computer establishes contact with another station, acknowledges responses, and even, supposedly, holds a "conversation" by playing prerecorded tapes. The purpose behind all of this escapes me. Apparently, it is little more than a contest to see which radio operator can make the most contacts in this manner. Well, we are talking about games, after all.

Virtually any game that can be played by any means can be translated into a computerized version. Some kinds of games, such as chess, seem better suited to computer adaptations than others, such as golf. But I have seen a computer golf game. Apparently, individual taste, imagination, creativity, and enthusiasm for the game are stronger determining factors for its adaptation to computer than mere logic. One caveat applies to games: Computer games available as adjuncts to more-serious computer uses can be amusing and entertaining diversions, but if you are considering buying a general-purpose computer primarily to provide yourself with a game opponent, first see if you can try the games on a friend's machine—and play them as many times as you can. While there is usually an initial gee-whiz reaction to computer games, they quickly tend to get dull. After you've played them a number of times, the computer's logic becomes predictable, and its repertoire of cute responses is limited. If you are an aficionado of chess or the arcade-type games, you might be better off to buy a games system that specializes in your particular interest. Otherwise, you will be paying for lots of computer that you might never use.

I tend to think of computerized games in three broad groupings: "think games," "adventure games," and "shoot-'em-ups," or the arcade-type video games. Think games are the ones that pit you against the computer's logic; adventure games are the ones that lead you through a variety of perils in quest of a goal; and the shoot-'em-ups are the microcomputer versions of the arcade games that usually go for a quarter a play. Each of these kinds of games has its own appeal, but some, I think, are more worthwhile than others.

● Think Games

Think games are the ones I consider most worthwhile, more for the writing of the programs than for the playing of the games. They occupy a continuum from the trivial, such as tic-tac-toe (to which nobody pays much attention), to the complex, such as chess (where tournaments are held for computer contestants and prizes are awarded). In between are card games such as cribbage and bridge, logic games such as Mastermind, and other board games such as Nine-Men's Morris, checkers, and Othello. Hallmarks of these games are

programmed logic against which the human logic must compete and, in the case of card games, the random chance of the deal.

There is little to say about the games themselves. They play, as you might imagine, with some degree of fidelity to their real-life models. You can find ready-to-go programs for many think games for most of the popular microcomputers, but nearly every amateur programmer I know has taken his crack at the ones that amuse him the most. While the game may be of little importance, writing it is excellent practice for more-serious programming. Much of the logic necessary to make the computer play the games is directly transferable to non-game programming. Practicing by writing game programs involves no risk from errors with real data, produces visible, known results, and can provide hours of challenging entertainment along with the inner satisfaction of success.

Whether or not you ever play the games you write is neither here nor there: The point is to write them. A friend of mine spent untold hours writing a checkers program. When it was finished, he played it several times to assure himself that it worked correctly, then put it on a shelf and hasn't touched it since. On the other hand, I have a cribbage program that I've used to while away odd hours for several years.

● Adventure Games

Adventure games typically place you, the adventurer, in some kind of situation in which you must battle fearsome creatures and avoid fatal pitfalls while you try to rescue an imprisoned princess or retrieve a hidden treasure. In order to do these things, you usually have to use clues and "objects" provided along the way to determine where to go and to help you to get there. Some of the adventure games drearily lead you through the same old haunted house or critter-infested cave time after time, and once you've solved the mystery, the game is over. Others, such as those of the fantasy role-playing variety, allow you to create a character with individual personality traits and physical characteristics and to take him again and again into constantly varying situations in which his success depends on his personality and experience.

The straightforward adventure games are relatively easy to write, once you get the hang of them, and there are even books on the market to help you create your own adventures. Probably the grandfather of all the adventure games is one that is trivial by current standards: Wumpus. The Wumpus is a creature nobody has ever seen that lives in a special cave containing bottomless pits and giant bats. The mission of the hunter is to find the Wumpus and shoot him with arrows that have the characteristic of being able to go around corners. As with the think games, writing one Wumpus program (and one is enough) is good practice. The Wumpus can be individualized to suit your tastes—my own is a slightly scatological fellow who never fails to draw a reaction from the uninitiated.

● **Arcade Games**

Arcade games are exciting because of their ability to transport the player into a fantasy (usually science fiction) world, their need for quick decisions and responses, and the thrill of the battle. If arcade games are your cup of tea, you probably would be best off to pick a computer having high-resolution color graphics and a wide variety of the games all set to go. If you want to try your hand at writing one, be prepared to invest some time in the project. While the arcade games are not technically or mathematically difficult to write, they are tedious, because you have to keep track of every planet, space ship, laser shot, and piece of debris on the screen. In order to achieve the speeds at which the im-

ages move with all the housekeeping that has to be done, the programs must be written in machine code (assembly language) or at least with a compiler (and even a compiled version might not be fast enough). Programming in assembly language requires a good deal of knowledge about how your computer works, and is not a skill that is attained overnight. A compiler program costs about two hundred dollars, and with most of them, the high-level-language program must be carefully structured, or, in other words, you have to know a good deal about how your high-level language works.

● **Models and Simulations**

Models and simulations substitute the computer for the real thing. In the real world, they are used where time, money, or dangerous situations prohibit performing actual experiments or building prototypes, such as wind-tunnel experiments, nuclear-fusion power generation, or nuclear-fission explosions. Under most circumstances, the models you might attempt on a hobby microcomputer would be on a more modest scale (but who knows?).

Models are also used where an actual situation cannot be found or created, such as in queuing problems. For example, given a customer load in a retail store, how many clerks distributed in what way will result in how much waiting time for the customers, with what effect on profits? In actuality, either a "model" customer distribution would never exist or it would take months of gathering data to see what really happened. With a computer model, you can vary the number of customers and the number of clerks, quickly get results, and adjust the variables to optimize customer waiting time and the cost of hiring additional employees.

One hobby "simulation" that's made the rounds is called Dragster. It's a computerized drag race. The program contains the design parameters for an optimized dragster, and you are offered the opportunity to "design" your own dragster and pit it against the built-in one. I put simulation in quotes in the first sentence of this paragraph because simulations involve real time: Dragster typically takes ten to fifteen minutes to run a race that in reality lasts only a minute or two.

Models can be entertaining, instructive, and, depending on your interests, profitable. Suppose that you've invented a new system for blackjack: Trying it in casinos would take a lot of time and could be costly if you'd overlooked something. But a computer model would allow you to test your theory, tally the occurrences of situations in the game, and so forth.

Like so many other microcomputer applications, models and simulations are limited only by your interests, ingenuity, and creativity.

• Artificial Intelligence

Artificial intelligence (AI) is one of the last real frontiers in computer science. Chess playing and other forms of "expert" systems are one variety; others are speech and pattern recognition, robotics, and problem solving.

While computers easily outstrip human abilities in performing repeated mathematical computations and other such mechanical chores, they don't do well in situations that human beings accept as routine—literally without a second thought. Handling badly mangled speech is one example: Humans easily unscramble ungrammatical sentences and translate metaphors that drive computers nuts. (The classic example is a computer translation of the saying "out of sight, out of mind." "Invisible, insane," the computer said.) Despite massive data bases, computers can't recognize meaningless questions. A human would laugh if asked, "What kind of microcomputer did Pythagoras use?" A computer would plod through all its files only to find that it didn't have that information.

The field of artificial intelligence is fresh and dynamic, and the literature on it is plentiful and readily available. The point about AI here is this: In its thirty-year history, it hasn't changed much. Computers have gotten bigger and faster, and new programming languages and techniques have been developed, but much of AI still hangs on concepts that haven't kept pace with technology. There have been no real breakthroughs. It has been suggested by one AI expert that the breakthrough could come from an amateur dabbling with his 16K microcomputer on the kitchen table in his apartment. You could still be the one to make that breakthrough.

• Combining Hobbies

It seems that the computer hobbyists whose interest remains strongest after the initial novelty of their machines has worn off are those who integrate their computer activities with other hobbies. Amateur radio has already been suggested as a natural combination with computers. Amateur astronomy is another. Programs currently available will let you compose music at a computer, hear the notes as they're entered, display the score on a screen, and print out a page of music when you're ready.

One friend uses his microcomputer to digest race information and help him handicap horses; another uses hers in genealogical work; another uses his to tally sports-car-rally results; still another uses her color computer to create needlework patterns.

If you have a major hobby or interest you've pursued for a long time, it's likely that you could enhance both your old hobby and a new one by combining the two of them.

GLOSSARY

This glossary serves two purposes. First, it is, I hope, a handy reference for the terminology that appears throughout this book. Its second aim, however, is to acquaint you with computer terminology that you are likely to encounter when reading about computers or talking to people involved with them. Included are a number of terms that are not strictly applicable to microcomputers but are so common in computerese that they are worth knowing.

This glossary, then, is a quick and handy dictionary. But don't confine its use to reference purposes. Start with the first entry and read through the glossary once, just to familiarize yourself with computer talk.

ACCESS MEMORY: To remove a word from memory and store it temporarily in a CPU register.

ACCESS TIME: The time that elapses between a call for data from a storage device and the availability of that data.

ACCUMULATOR: One of several registers that temporarily store, or "accumulate," the results of various operations.

ADAPTER: Any device through which two or more units, not otherwise compatible, can be made to operate together. See *interface*.

ADDER: An electronic circuit that adds two numbers together.

ADDRESS: The designation of a specific location in memory or of an I/O device.

ADDRESS BUS: A line along which the address is transmitted from the central processing unit to memory and I/O peripherals.

ADDRESS REGISTER: A register used for storing an address.

ADD TIME: The length of time it takes for a microprocessor to add two numbers of several digits. The relative speed of a microprocessor is often given in terms of add time.

ALGORITHM: A sequence of operations, either mathematical or logical, or both, which, when followed, achieves a predictable result such as a solution to a problem, an operation, or the establishment of a set of circumstances.

ALPHANUMERICS: The Roman alphabet in upper and lower case and the digits 0 through 9.

ALU: Abbreviation for arithmetic/logic unit.

ANSI: American National Standards Institute, an organization dedicated to the establishment of industrial standards, including standards for computers.

APPLICATION SOFTWARE: See *software*.

ARCHITECTURE: Literally, the structure of a computer system. The term involves the physical hardware, the manner and order in which processing is performed, the arrangement of the elements of a computer, even the circuitry on the chips. The bus, storage, and control capacities of a microcomputer are all parts of its architecture.

ARITHMETIC/LOGIC UNIT (ALU): That portion of a central processing unit where the mathematical and logical operations are carried out.

ASCII: Acronym for *A*merican *S*tandard *C*ode for *I*nformation *I*nterchange. This code, widely used by microcomputers for the transmission of data between a central processing unit and its I/O peripherals, consists of 128 letters, numbers, punctuation marks, and special symbols, each of which consists of a binary pattern that uses seven binary digits. The remaining bit, called a parity bit, is used to detect certain errors.

ASSEMBLER: A software program that converts symbolic or mnemonic language into machine language.

ASSEMBLY LANGUAGE: A programming language that uses mnemonics to show what each instruction does when it is carried out. Assembly language requires more knowledge and skill than so-called high-level language, but is easier to use than machine language.

ASYNCHRONOUS: When the data signals between two or more units of equipment are not timed by the frequency of a common clock, they are said to be asynchronous. When such an asynchronous state exists, it is handled by a process known as handshaking (which see).

BASIC: Acronym for *B*eginner's *A*ll-purpose *S*ymbolic *I*nstruction *C*ode—a high-level programming language that is particularly popular among users of microcomputers be-

cause of its relative simplicity for programming.

BATCH PROCESSING: The processing of data that has been input at some time prior to the time that the actual processing is being performed. See *real time*.

BAUD: A unit by which signal speeds are measured. In microprocessing, the baud rate refers to the number of bits per second.

BCD: Abbreviation for binary coded decimal.

BCD-TO-DECIMAL CONVERTER: An inexpensive integrated circuit chip that changes BCD to the decimal system. (Sometimes called a decoder.)

BENCHMARK: A test program or test problem used to make comparisons between computers. Criteria may be speed, memory requirements, costs, ease of programming, etc.

BINARY: A number system that has 2 as its base and that uses only the digits 0 and 1. The binary notation system is used by digital computers to perform the various tasks that are involved in data processing.

BINARY CODED DECIMAL (BCD): A system in which a binary code is used to represent a decimal number.

BINARY-TO-BCD CONVERSION: The conversion of a binary number into its equivalent in BCD.

BINARY-TO-DECIMAL CONVERSION: The conversion of a binary number into its equivalent decimal number.

BINARY-TO-HEXADECIMAL CONVERSION: The conversion of a binary number into its equivalent number in the hexadecimal (i.e., base-16) system.

BIT: Contraction of *bi*nary dig*it*.

BIT RATE: The number of bits transmitted per second.

BITS PER INCH (BPI): A measurement of the number of positions per linear inch of some recording medium—such as magnetic tape—which can contain one bit of information.

BLOCK DIAGRAM: A fairly simple drawing showing the layout of a computer system. The major components are indicated by rectangles, which are connected by straight lines. A typical block diagram for a microcomputer will include the CPU, ROM, RAM, the I/O interface, and the clock. Arrows are drawn to show the direction of the flow of data. The purchaser of a complete computer system will find a block diagram useful in visualizing the basic contents of the box and their various functions. Someone who wants to develop his own system will almost certainly need to begin with a block diagram.

BOOLEAN LOGIC: Mathematical logic processes based on a system of algebra developed in the early-nineteenth century by English mathematician George Boole. Boolean logic plays a significant part in the various functions and operations performed by a computer.

BOOTSTRAP: A term used to describe either a device or a technique that brings itself into a desired state by means of an action it performs itself. For example, a bootstrap loader is a short program for the first few steps of a program designed to load the rest of the program into the computer.

BPI: Abbreviation for bits per inch.

BPS: Abbreviation for bits per second.

BRANCH INSTRUCTION: A programming instruction that causes the computer to discontinue the sequential program instructions and move to another location in memory. The major types of branch instructions are "branch-on-condition" and "branch-unconditional." The branch-on-condition instruction tells the computer to perform a branch when some specified condition occurs. The branch-unconditional instruction always requires a transfer to another part of the program when this instruction is reached.

BREADBOARD: In the jargon of microcomputers, a breadboard is a fixture on which electronic circuitry that is being worked on is mounted. "To breadboard" is to spread out the circuitry so as to facilitate its assembly and testing.

BUG: A defect or an error, in either the hardware or the software, which causes the system to malfunction. See *debug*.

BULK STORAGE: Memory units in which large amounts of data may be stored. This data is transferred to the bulk-storage equipment from the main memory of a computer and may be recalled later as needed.

BUS: A conductor, or a set of conductors in parallel, used to transmit data, signals, or power between parts of a computer system.

BUS DRIVER: An electronic amplifier designed to provide sufficient power to either control or activate electronic circuits that are connected to a great many devices. (Sometimes called line driver.)

BUS SYSTEM: All the buses in a computer system that connect the computer to its peripherals.

BYTE: Eight bits. Most microcomputers use data words of eight bits, so in microprocessing, byte is generally synonymous with "word."

CAGE: A chassis used for mounting printed circuit cards. (Also known as "card cage.")

CARD: A board with a printed circuit; also a punched card (which see).

CARD EXTENDER: A device that enables a card to be removed from its chassis for testing. The card is plugged into the extender, and the extender is then plugged into the space previously occupied by the card. This raises the card above the other cards and permits examination and testing.

CARD PUNCH: A device that records information by punching holes in cards. The holes represent letters, digits, and special characters.

CARD READER: A device that senses the holes in punched cards and translates them into machine code.

CATHODE-RAY TUBE (CRT): An electronic vacuum tube, such as a television picture tube, that can be used to display graphic images. CRT terminals are popular I/O devices for microcomputers.

CELL: A memory location that may be capable of storing only one bit, but this usually refers to a register capable of storing a word or instruction.

CENTRAL PROCESSING UNIT (CPU): A unit of a computer that handles the decoding and execution of instructions, controls the use of memory, performs arithmetic functions, etc. The CPU, which usually consists of an arithmetic/logic unit (ALU), several special temporary registers, and control circuitry, is the heart of a computer system.

CHARACTER: Anything that is used to represent, organize, or transmit data; it may be a letter of the alphabet, a digit, a punctuation mark, or any special symbol (such as the plus sign or the equals sign).

CHIP: A very small silicon wafer containing an integrated circuit.

CLOCK: A device that generates electronic pulses by which all the components of a computer system are synchronized. "Clock" also refers to the series of pulses themselves.

CLOCK PULSE (CP): The synchronization signal, which is the time unit within a computer system.

CODE: A set of unique symbols used to represent data, or information, and the rules setting forth the way in which those symbols can be used.

CODER: An electronic circuit that encodes.

COMPILER: A program that converts a program written in a high-level language into machine language.

CONDITIONAL JUMP: Branch-on-condition. See *branch instruction*.

CONSOLE: The control panel of the computer, which permits the operator to use the system.

CONTROL BLOCK: The electronic circuitry in the central processing unit that performs the control function; also, a storage area used by a program to hold control information.

CONTROLLER: An adapter that permits the control of an I/O device by the central processing unit.

CONVERTER: Electronic circuitry, or a device, that converts data from one code into another code.

CORE MEMORY: A main storage device comprising tiny magnetic cores looped around the intersections in a grid of fine wires. Not many microcomputers—if any—use core memory, but a great many larger systems do.

CP: Abbreviation for clock pulse.

CPU: Abbreviation for central processing unit.

CROM: Acronym for *Control Read-Only Memory*, a part of most CPU chips. The CROM is the storage area for detailed instructions assembled by the CPU to enable the performance of more-complex instructions such as addition, subtraction, etc.

CRT: Abbreviation for cathode-ray tube.

DATA: Basically, data is information. It must be arranged first in a manner that enables it to be communicated to a computer, and second, in a form that the computer can operate on, or "process." Everything that goes into a computer may be classified as data, but, generally, the term "instructions" refers to those words that tell the computer what to do, and "data" refers to the information that is to be processed.

DATA BASE: The total quantity of data that is available to a computer for making calculations and decisions. IBM defines data base as "a collection of data fundamental to an enterprise."

DATA BUS: See *bus*.

DATA POINTER: A CPU register that temporarily holds the address of the next byte that is to be brought from memory.

DATA PROCESSING: The performance of a systematic sequence of operations—mathematical, logical, or both—which a computer performs on data.

DATA RETRIEVAL: The bringing of data from storage—typically, bulk storage—to a location where it can be used or processed.

DEBUG: To seek out the source of errors or malfunctions, in computer hardware or in a program, that prevent the efficient or normal operation of the program or the computer system and correct them. It is also the name of a program sometimes used for troubleshooting. See *bug*.

DECIMAL-TO-BCD CONVERSION: The conversion of a decimal number to its equivalent binary-coded-decimal number.

DECIMAL-TO-BINARY CONVERSION: The conversion of a decimal number to its equivalent binary (base-2) number.

DECIMAL-TO-HEXADECIMAL CONVERSION: The conversion of a decimal number to its equivalent hexadecimal (base-16) number.

DECODE: To translate from one code to another; also, to translate data back into the language in which it was originally written.

DECODER: A device or system used to decode.

DEDICATION: The assignment of a program, an I/O device, or an entire system to a single application or purpose.

DISK: A plate resembling a phonograph record and coated with magnetic material on which data may be "recorded" in great quantities for subsequent retrieval. "Floppy" disks are flexible and somewhat less costly to use. There are floppy-disk storage units that are compatible with microcomputers. These tend to be somewhat expensive and are best suited for business applications.

DISKETTE: A "floppy" disk. See *disk*.

DISK OPERATING SYSTEM (DOS): Contains the system programming that makes the diskette drives work, and utility programs for system management, and may either enhance the operating-system stores in the computer's ROM or control system operation in lieu of ROM.

DOCUMENTATION: All the written material that is necessary to establish and operate a computer system. This includes (but is not necessarily limited to) the instruction manual, maintenance information, program descriptions, etc.

DOWN: When a computer system or one of its components is unable to function because of a programming error, a power failure, or a repair or maintenance problem, the system or component is said to be "down." Compare *up and running*.

DOWNLOAD: To hold or store incoming information. See *upload*.

DUMP: A printout of the contents of a section of memory. "To dump" is to render such a printout.

DYNAMIC STORAGE: A highly volatile memory that requires recharging at regular intervals to prevent the loss of data. See *volatility*.

EAROM: Acronym for *E*lectrically *A*lterable *R*ead-*O*nly *M*emory, a ROM whose automatic erasure can be programmed. See *PROM* and *ROM*.

EBCDIC: Acronym for *E*xtended *B*inary *C*oded *D*ecimal *I*nter*C*hange, a character code widely used by computers.

EDIT: To change portions of a computer program or data by making insertions, deletions, or corrections.

EDITOR: A program or a portion of a program designed for a specific computer to be used for editing. The editor simplifies insertions and deletions by automatically renumbering the instructions and then producing a new program listing with the revisions.

EDP: Abbreviation for electronic data processing.

EPROM: Acronym for *E*rasable *P*rogrammable *Read-Only Memory*. Like other PROMs, an EPROM can be electrically programmed. However, using an ultraviolet light, that program can be erased and another program entered.

EXECUTIVE PROGRAM: A program that controls or supervises the execution of other programs or the overall operation of a system.

EXPANSION CARD: A card on which chips or circuits can be mounted. The card is then added to the system to expand its capability.

FIELD: The collection of characters that represent one basic unit of information.

FILE: The collection of all records associated with one activity in a data base.

FIRMWARE: A program that has been implanted in a read-only memory (ROM) device.

FLAG: In microcomputers, a register that indicates the existence of a particular condition in the computer system.

FLIP-FLOP: An electronic circuit of two opposite polarities, the interchange of which is controlled by a signal from the clock. A number of elements of a microcomputer use flip-flops, including flag registers.

FLOPPY DISK: See *disk*.

FLOPPY-DISK DRIVE: A device that permits the CPU to write to or read from a floppy disk. (Sometimes called a "loader.")

FLOWCHART: A diagram showing the "flow," or sequential steps, of a computer program.

HALF-ADDER: One of the two components of an adder.

HANDSHAKING: Signals or pulses that establish synchronization between an asynchronous I/O unit and the computer.

HARD COPY: A computer's output that is printed on paper.

HARDWARE: The physical components of a computer system: the electronics, the wires, the plastic, the glass, and the metal. (Compare firmware, software.)

HEX: Hexadecimal.

HEXADECIMAL NUMBER SYSTEM: A number system that uses 16 as its base. A hexadecimal code is used as a shorthand method of writing lengthy binary words or numbers.

HIGH-LEVEL LANGUAGE: A computer programming language that is easy and convenient for the programmer. The computer can convert the high-level language to machine language. BASIC is the most common high-level language used with microcomputers.

HITS: Acronym for *Hobbyist's Interchange Tape Standard*, a data-recording format that utilizes tape cassettes and is designed to permit an interchange of cassettes and programs among some hobbyists.

IC: Abbreviation for integrated circuit.

INFORMATION RETRIEVAL: See *data retrieval*.

INPUT: A signal emanating from a peripheral device and going into the central processing unit. Also, "to input" is to place data into the data processing system. Also, the data itself.

INPUT/OUTPUT (I/O) DEVICE: Any peripheral hardware used to input data to the computer or take data (output) from the computer. I/O devices may be CRT terminals, printers, various storage devices, etc.

INPUT PORT: See *I/O port*.

INTEGRATED CIRCUIT (IC): A complete electronic circuit contained on a minute chip of silicon. Integrated circuits may consist of only a few transistors, resistors, diodes, capacitors, etc., or thousands of them. They are generally classified, according to the complexity of the circuitry, as Small-Scale Integration (SSI), Medium-Scale Integration (MSI), Large-Scale Integration (LSI), and Very-Large-Scale Integration (VLSI).

INTERFACE: The place or boundary line

where two pieces of equipment or hardware meet. An interface is also a piece of hardware —an adapter—that makes two pieces of equipment compatible. "Interface" is sometimes used as a verb.

INTERNAL MEMORY: A computer's main, high-speed memory, which is contained within the computer, as opposed to peripheral bulk storage.

INTERPRETER: A compiler program that converts one instruction at a time into machine language.

INTERRUPT: A signal from an I/O device to the central processing unit requesting some form of action. Through a series of procedures, the CPU interrupts the program it is following and attends to the task called for by the interrupt signal. The CPU then returns to the execution of its program.

I/O: Abbreviation for input/output.

I/O DEVICE: See *input/output device*.

I/O PORT: A port designed for use in conjunction with an I/O device. See *port*.

JUMP: See *branch instruction*.

K: Abbreviation for the prefix kilo- (of Greek origin), meaning one thousand. A kilometer is a thousand meters. Computer memory is given in terms of thousands of bytes, or kilobytes; 8,000 bytes=8 kilobytes=8K.

KEYBOARD: The typewriter-like portion of an I/O device, such as a CRT terminal or a teletypewriter. Also often used to designate the numerical keyboard of a calculator, although that is more commonly referred to as a keypad.

KEYPAD: See *keyboard*.

KILOBAUD: A thousand bauds.

KILOBIT: A thousand bits.

KILOBYTE: A thousand bytes.

LABEL: An alphabetical, numerical, or symbolic means of identifying specific memory addresses or locations in a program.

LANGUAGE: Any system of communication of ideas and information that uses a set of fixed symbols in accordance with specific rules. Computer languages permit communication between people and computers.

LARGE-SCALE INTEGRATION (LSI): See *integrated circuit*.

LED: Abbreviation for light-emitting diode, a semiconducting electronic device which, as part of an I/O device, displays letters or numbers in a readout that is usually red or green.

LIGHT PEN: An input device resembling a pen and containing a photocell and photomultiplier. It is used for "writing" on a CRT.

LINE DRIVER: Synonymous with bus driver.

LIQUID CRYSTAL DISPLAY (LCD): A type of readout used in I/O devices; many digital watches and quite a few hand-held calculators now use LCDs in preference to LEDs.

LOAD: To enter data into a computer's memory or registers.

LOADER: A computer program that takes another program from storage and loads it into the computer.

LOCATION: The memory cell in which a data word or instruction is stored.

LOGIC CIRCUITRY: The hardware that performs logical operations.

LOGICAL EXPRESSION: A logical relationship expressed in Boolean algebra.

LOOP: A set of computer instructions carried out repeatedly until some condition occurs that instructs the computer to discontinue the looping process.

LSI: Abbreviation for large-scale integration. See *integrated circuit*.

MACHINE CODE: Synonymous with machine language (which see).

MACHINE LANGUAGE: A language consisting of a binary code. Computers "understand" only machine language, so all other programming languages must be converted to machine language prior to being entered into the CPU.

MAGNETIC CORE: See *core memory*.

MAGNETIC TAPE: Basically, recording tape of the type used in tape recorders. For expensive, large computers, the magnetic oxide material with which the plastic tape is coated may differ somewhat to conform to the specific purpose for which the tape is to be used. Among microcomputer users, however, the tape cassette has become a popular means of bulk storage, and the inexpensive variety available almost anywhere has proved both economical and useful. Magnetic tape is sometimes called "mag" tape.

MAINFRAME: Three sources offer three definitions of "mainframe." One source claims that the word refers to the computer itself— i.e., the CPU and memory—and specifically excludes peripherals. Another source claims that mainframe is synonymous with central processing unit. The third source claims that the mainframe is the computer chassis holding the printed circuit cards. They are all more or less correct, depending on context.

MAINFRAME SLOT: A slot in the chassis of a microcomputer in which PC cards are placed. Many microcomputers have empty slots, which allow for subsequent expansion of the system.

MASS STORAGE DEVICE: A kind of electronic file cabinet which retains large quantities of data from a computer's memory for possible later retrieval.

MEDIUM-SCALE INTEGRATION (MSI): See *integrated circuit*.

MEGA-: A prefix (from the Greek) meaning one million. A megabyte is a million bytes.

MEMORY: The facility in a computer which holds a certain amount of information that the CPU can directly inspect, modify if required, and store again for later use. See *storage*.

MEMORY ALLOCATION: The designation of memory cells for a specific purpose.

MEMORY PROTECTION: A means of protecting against the loss of data from memory. Memory protection may be hardware, firmware, or software. Memory can be lost through power failure, through variations in current or voltage, or by accidentally "overwriting." This is comparable to recording over a magnetic tape and, in so doing, erasing the data previously recorded on that tape.

METAL OXIDE SEMICONDUCTOR (MOS): A type of transistor technology widely used in microcomputer systems.

MICRO-: A prefix (from the Greek) that means "small" or one millionth, depending on context. It is often signified by the Greek letter *mu,* which looks like this: μ. Because of the absence of this symbol in most typewriters and type fonts, "micro" is frequently and erroneously represented by a lower case *u.*

MICROCOMPUTER: A small computer whose CPU is an integrated circuit embedded in a semiconductor chip. Integrated-circuit technology has made it possible to develop small computers with enormous capabilities.

MICROPROCESSOR: A central processing unit that comprises one or several semiconductor chips.

MICROSECOND: A millionth of a second; abbreviated μsec or (erroneously) usec.

MILLISECOND: A thousandth of a second; abbreviated ms.

MINICOMPUTER: A computer that is larger than a microcomputer but smaller than a big computer. (For some reason, one never hears the term "maxicomputer.") Whether a computer is a mini or a micro depends somewhat on price and memory size. There are, however, no clear-cut distinctions between the two categories.

MODEM: Acronym for *MO*dulator/ *DEM*odulator, a device that converts data so that it can be transmitted over communications (e.g., telephone) lines, or reconverts data at the receiving end.

MOS: See *metal oxide semiconductor*.

MOTHERBOARD: An assembly board on which printed circuits can be interconnected through a bus.

MPU: Abbreviation for microprocessor unit or microprocessing unit; analogous to *CPU* (which see).

MSI: Abbreviation for medium-scale integration. See *integrated circuit*.

NANOSECOND: A billionth of a second.

NIBBLE: Half a byte; a word consisting of four bits. Sometimes spelled "nybble."

NUMBER-CRUNCHING: Descriptive of a computer or a program whose purpose is to perform large quantities of arithmetical computations.

NYBBLE: See *nibble*.

OBJECT PROGRAM: A program that has been translated into a form readable by the computer. Compare *source program*.

ONLINE: A peripheral unit operating in conjunction with a computer is said to be online.

OUTPUT: The data that a computer transmits to a peripheral device. Also used as a verb: "to output."

PAPER TAPE: See *punched tape*.

PARALLEL-TO-SERIES CONVERTER: Circuitry that takes data being fed in parallel (i.e., along several pathways simultaneously) and converts it to serial transmission (i.e., over a single pathway). Compare *series-to-parallel converter*.

PARALLEL TRANSMISSION: The transmission of data along several pathways at the same time. Compare *serial transmission*.

PARITY: The odd or even number of 1's in a binary word, byte, character, or message. The importance of parity is in its use as a code for detecting errors.

PC CARD or BOARD: See *printed circuit card*.

PERFORATED TAPE: See *punched tape*.

PERIPHERAL: Descriptive of devices that work in conjunction with, but are not part of, the computer, such as CRT terminals, teletypewriters, printers, tape recorders, etc. Often the word is used as a noun and one speaks of such a device as "a peripheral."

PIN: A connection terminal of an integrated circuit.

PORT: A terminal through which data goes into or comes out of a computer.

PRINTED CIRCUIT (PC) CARD: A card made of plastic material onto which electronic components and circuitry are mounted. Sometimes called a "PC board."

PRINTER: Any one of several peripherals delivering hard-copy printouts of computerized data.

PRINTOUT: The output of a printer. Also used as a verb: "to print out."

PROCESSOR: A program that provides for compilation, translation, and various other functions of a specific programming language. Also, a "processor" is anything that does processing.

PROGRAM: For computers, a program is a set of sequential instructions designed to achieve a specific result, and which a computer is capable of accepting. Also, "to program" is to write such a set of instructions.

PROGRAMMER: A person who designs, writes, and tests programs. (However, these separate functions are sometimes performed by several people.)

PROM: Acronym for *Programmable Read-Only Memory*, a read-only memory that the user of a microcomputer can program himself, using a device known as a PROM burner. PROMs that can be erased and reprogrammed are known as EROMs (*Erasable Read-Only Memories*) or EPROMs (*Erasable Programmable Read-Only Memories*). See *ROM*.

PROM BURNER: A device that "etches"

programs into PROMs; also called a PROM programmer.

PULSE: An electrical signal of rapidly alternating voltage levels, used to transmit data.

PUNCHED CARD: A card on which holes have been punched to represent letters, digits, and special characters. The holes are sensed by a card reader, which translates the data represented by the holes into machine code.

PUNCHED TAPE: A Mylar or paper strip approximately an inch wide, onto which data is encoded by means of a series of holes punched into the tape.

RAM: Acronym for random-access memory.

RANDOM-ACCESS MEMORY (RAM): A computer memory that has been arranged into cells, any one of which can be "accessed" directly, rather than having to go through cells sequentially to reach the one that is desired. In a microcomputer, RAM refers to read/write memory that serves as a scratch pad, a temporary place to hold data, partial results, program instructions, etc.

READOUT: A display on an LED, LCD, CRT, or other visual device.

REAL TIME: A term that describes the processing of data as soon as it is received. Compare *batch processing*.

RECORD: All the fields associated with the key item of interest in a data base.

REGISTER: A temporary memory location in a microcomputer.

RETRIEVAL: See *data retrieval*.

ROM: Acronym for *Read-Only Memory*. Computer memory that can be read but cannot be written to. The pattern of a ROM is fixed and unalterable and is therefore useful for fixed data, program instructions, etc. Compare *EPROM* and *PROM*.

ROUTINE: A set of instructions to be carried out in sequence by the computer for the purpose of achieving a specific function. A routine is a kind of program within a program. (It is sometimes called a "subroutine.")

SCRATCH-PAD MEMORY: See *Random-Access Memory*.

SEMICONDUCTOR: An element, usually silicon or germanium, which, when diffused with certain impurities, becomes a carrier of positive or negative electrical charges. Semiconductor technology has made possible the manufacture of minuscule electrical circuits, giving rise to microprocessors and several important new industries.

SERIAL TRANSMISSION: The transmission of data over a single pathway. Compare *parallel transmission*.

SERIES-TO-PARALLEL CONVERTER: A register that accepts data in series and outputs that data in parallel. Compare *parallel-to-series converter*.

SMALL-SCALE INTEGRATION (SSI): See *integrated circuit*.

SOFTWARE: A computer's programs. System software includes programs that enable the system to function, such as compilers, assemblers, interpreters, executive programs, etc. Application software usually refers to programs intended to solve problems or produce results. Also, many microcomputer users consider software to be anything that does not qualify as hardware or firmware.

SOURCE LANGUAGE: The language in which a program is written. If the source language is high-level, then it will be translated into object language.

SOURCE PROGRAM: A program that has been written in source language and will be converted to an object program.

SSI: Abbreviation for small-scale integration. See *integrated circuit*.

STORAGE: A known place to store information, not directly accessible in a computer's memory, such as on a magnetic tape, disk, or diskette. See *memory*.

SUBROUTINE: A portion of a program or a routine that may be used repeatedly during a program. See *routine*.

SYMBOLIC LANGUAGE: A programming language that uses a mnemonic code.

SYSTEM: A group of elements that interact to form an entity. A computer system minimally consists of a central processing unit, an input device, and an output device. Other components may be added to the system as needed.

SYSTEMS ANALYST: A person who analyzes a system in order to make improvements or solve problems.

TAPE: Punched tape or magnetic tape.

TAPE CASSETTE: A cassette containing magnetic recording tape. It is one of the most economical and, therefore, one of the most popular bulk storage media for microcomputers.

TAPE PUNCH: A device that makes the holes in punched tape.

TAPE READER: A device that reads the holes in punched tape and enters the data into the computer.

TEMPLATE: A plastic stencil for flowchart symbols.

TEXT EDITOR: See *editor*.

THROUGHPUT RATE: The speed with which a computer processes data and produces a result.

TIME SHARING: A term that describes the simultaneous use of a central processing unit by two or more users, often remote from the CPU and each other. Actually, the simultaneity is an illusion. The CPU is handling each I/O sequentially, but with such incredible speed that delays are barely perceptible (except when heavy demands are made on a large computer).

TTY: Abbreviation for teletypewriter.

u: A substitute for the symbol μ, the Greek letter *mu,* which stands for micro-.

uC: Abbreviation for microcomputer.

uP: Abbreviation for microprocessor.

UP AND RUNNING: When a computer or one of its components has been "down" and is restored to full operation, it is said to be "up and running."

UPLOAD: To automatically transmit information previously stored when you are not hooked up to the telephone. See *download*.

VERY-LARGE-SCALE INTEGRATION (VLSI): See *integrated circuit*.

VIDEO: In microcomputers, descriptive of any terminal that uses a CRT screen, such as a television set.

VIRTUAL MEMORY: A technique that uses disk or diskette in a way that makes the computer appear to have much more memory than its inherent addressing capability would permit.

VLSI: Very-large-scale integration. See *integrated circuit*.

VOLATILITY: The condition of memories and registers that lose their data when power is turned off or interrupted. Also, certain memories and registers that must be continually refreshed by the power supply to prevent the loss of data are said to be volatile.

WORD: A group of characters that the computer treats as a single unit.

WORD LENGTH: The number of bits that make up a word. Most microcomputers use 8-bit words; therefore "byte" and "word" are used interchangeably.

WRITE: To enter data into memory or a register or onto an output medium such as tape or paper.